"*Quadratos* gives us a map of faith that allows Christianity to move forward in new and constructive ways, yet keeps us firmly anchored in the Gospels and in our history. This is exactly the clarifying and transformative message we need to hear at this moment."
—*Bishop David G. Mullen,*
Lutheran Sierra Pacific Synod, ELCA

"This lyrical, passionate book takes one of the world's great sacred scriptures and offers it as the map of the universal spiritual journey, the transformation from the isolated suffering of the separate self to the liberation of selfless, shared compassion. What a gift for us all."
—*Sylvia Boorstein, meditation teacher and bestselling author –*
It's Easier Than You Think: The Buddhist Way to Happiness

"Dr. Shaia has cut through all the scriptural controversies to the deep places of wisdom. He confirms what my heart has always known."
—*Rev. George Wenzinger, Roman Catholic pastor*

"This is a wonderfully wise and profound vision of the Gospels, illuminating their inner meaning and our inner lives with them."
—*Jack Kornfield, co-founder of Spirit Rock Meditation*
Center and bestselling author – A Path with Heart:
A Guide through the Perils and Promises of Spiritual Life

"As a Jew and psychiatrist, I find Dr. Shaia's work to be a comprehensive understanding of the Gospels, and useful template for psychological growth."
—*Lawrence Greenberg, M.D., Professor Emeritus and Former*
Director of Child and Adolescent, Psychiatry, the School of
Medicine, University of Minnesota

BEYOND THE BIOGRAPHY OF JESUS:

THE JOURNEY OF QUADRATOS

BOOK I

ALEXANDER J. SHAIA

Cold Tree Press
Nashville, Tennessee

All scripture quoted, unless otherwise noted, is from, The New Oxford Annotated Bible (NRSV), Third Edition, Oxford University Press, 2001.

Jan L. Richardson, "I am not asking you." From In Wisdom's Path: Discovering the Sacred in Every Season. (Cleveland: The Pilgrim Press, 2000), 54. Copyright © 2000 by Jan L. Richardson. Used by permission.

Jan L. Richardson, "Warning." From In Wisdom's Path: Discovering the Sacred in Every Season. (Cleveland: The Pilgrim Press, 2000), 57. Copyright © 2000 by Jan L. Richardson. Used by permission.

"Psalm 121", "Psalm 22", from OPENING TO YOU by Norman Fischer, copyright © 2002 by Norman Fischer. Used by permission of Viking Penguin, a division of Penguin Group (USA) Inc.

Quote on frontispiece, from Adversus haereses, III, xi, 8, Bishop Irenaeus, 180 CE.

The term QUADRATOS and the accompanying logo ⊕ are registered trademarks.

Author Photo by JR Lancaster

Published by Cold Tree Press
Nashville, Tennessee
www.coldtreepress.com

DEDICATION

For those who have witnessed
from before the beginning

Larry and Carol,
Linda and Bob,
J.L. and Sharon,
Michelle, Connie

and
in memory of

Eva Maria Sanchez

Your pattern is perfection
It quiets the soul that knows it
And its eloquent expression
Makes everything clear
So that even the simple are wise

—Psalm 19:8, translation by Norman Fischer

There is just one revelation, but it must have four accounts,
for natural and divine law is quadriform.

—Bishop Irenaeus, 180 CE

TABLE OF CONTENTS

B o o k   I

INTRODUCTION

Quick Reference Guide to Quadratos

Note from the Author: This introduction is a quick summary of quadratos. You may wish to read it, mark it for reference, or move ahead where you will find the same information repeated in much greater detail. AJS

The Invitation

THIS BOOK AND its companion Book Two, offer a fresh, inspiring and pragmatic understanding of the four traditional Christian gospels—one that I think has been long awaited. In this book you will learn the untold story of *quadratos,* and why its underlying principle led the early Christian church to conclude that, out of all the choices they had, the four gospels of Matthew, Mark, John and Luke represented the greatest teaching that they could offer.

You will come to view the four traditional gospels differently than you ever have before. You will see them as a spiritual and psychological map that stretches across time, place and culture. This map restores the full process of spiritual transformation laid out by the early church and validates that ancient process through current under-standings of psychology, dramatically extending the curtailed versions offered in most Christian churches today. In this rediscovered and inspiring map, you will find a sequence of practices that gives purpose and meaning to life, transforming anxiety into equanimity, resentment into compassion, and loneliness into community and joy. This book will provide new and vital ways for you, your family and community to respond to unexpected dilemmas—and will do it without forsaking Christianity's sacred history and traditions.

This book addresses Christians as well as the many who are affected by, hurt by or interested in Christianity. For those of us who are believing Christians, we want to know that we can trust in the Gospels of Matthew, Mark, John and Luke, the core documents of the Christian faith, as revelations of divine truth. We want to understand if and how these sacred texts provide us a practical way to unite our hearts and minds in a faith we can live today, a time that is much more complex than village life millennia ago. This book gives us those truths. For non-Christians, this book offers a refreshing viewpoint on Christianity and may surprise non-Christians with its interesting history and usefulness as a practical guide to personal growth. Beyond the personal, the entire world needs increased maturity within the immense force of Christianity, and all faiths, so that our divisions might be healed.

To arrive at this rediscovered understanding of the gospels and put it into practice, we will move slowly, step by step, through an enormous terrain. As we move, for some, the ground will be entirely new. For those of us who have studied the gospels before, each small step may feel familiar. Yet each step will take us deeper into an ancient landscape. You may, at first, feel uncertain. Be patient. Trust that the treasure will be gradually revealed, and soon you will understand the pattern of *quadratos* and see the traditional four gospels shining—as they always have and always will—as the sacred scriptures of Christianity and the deep heart of God.

So many anxious questions have arisen from contemporary scholarship and popular fiction. We keep waiting for another piece of papyrus to be unearthed, or another translation or a new code. All of this will be put to rest in this book. Yes, of course it is true that these gospels are filled with historical discrepancies and have endured endless centuries of mistranslation. Yes, of course these gospels have been used to assert power and privilege, often unfairly.

Yes, these gospels have been at the center of theological and church debate. And although these matters are interesting and even important in some ways, this book will show that they do not affect in any way the truth of the gospels nor of quadratos. After taking this journey, you will be able to assert this yourself—through your own critical thought and with a full heart. You will know that the early Christians got it right—that Matthew, Mark, John and Luke are the four vital gospels that hold the great, over-arching message.

Quadratos Defined

Quadratos is my invented word for the sequential and unvarying four-fold pattern of spiritual and psychological growth found across all eras of human history, geography and cultures—and in the four gospels. Cyclical and ever deepening, it matches the rhythms of the four seasons, and of our lives. I have come to see the pattern of quadratos as omnipresent, and I think of it as the breath of God that moves within each person and through all of life.

Why these Four?

During the first and second centuries, at least fifty gospels were written. Yet by the end of the second century, holy teachers were stating that there must be *four* and only four accounts. Why not three or seven or fifty? What was so significant about this number that it would dictate the number of gospels taken into the official record? Because consciously aware or spiritually led, teachers of the time believed that natural and divine laws came in fours. Their word for this truth was "quadriform," and they believed that the truth of the spiritual pattern was more significant than the details of the biography of Jesus. Indeed, they considered the four gospels aspects of a single revelation.

Still, how did these four become the chosen four? There is no precise way to know. Scholarship today tells us that each of these four gospels was composed in response to the intense spiritual dilemma of a particular community that found itself in dire need. The gospel that was written was used for prayer and practice and provided hope and meaning in time of trial. For example, Mark, the first gospel composed, was written as the text for the Christians in Rome during the year they were summarily arrested and executed, condemned by Emperor Nero for setting the fire that destroyed the great city. Its metaphors and language are stark, appropriate for people under threat of death.

Each of the other three traditional gospels arose from a different time, a different community and a different dilemma, but each was just as compelling as that historical moment in Rome which gave birth to Mark. Yet we are still curious to know if the scholars who compiled the Bible in the succeeding centuries knew the history of those early communities, knew their spiritual questions and took that into account when they made decisions about what stayed in the final text, and in what order. Whether they did or not, it is likely that holy leaders did know the universal wisdom of the four-fold quadratos progression (begin, struggle, new wisdom, practice) since it had by that time been incorporated into the baptism ritual. So maybe they recognized its reflection in the four gospel stories and chose them. Or maybe, over time, these gospels were the natural choices that arose from the maturing Christian communities because when they prayed and studied those four texts so many lives were transformed. We will never know for certain, of course, but the result is so remarkable, that however the choosing and the compilation occurred, I am sure that Spirit led the process.

The Ancient Pattern

The debate over the exact way in which the four gospels—Matthew, Mark, John and Luke—were chosen isn't likely to stop any time soon. But once selected, the teachers and sages of those early centuries arranged the gospels in an odd, atypical, non-chronological sequence for prayer and reading and prescribed their use in an exact cycle of prayer and practice—one that precisely mirrors the way we spiritually and psychologically grow.

Christianity used that sequence as the invariable formal Sunday worship reading cycle for a thousand years, abandoned the sequence in the Middle Ages, and formally re-instated it in the 1970s and 80s. But until now, the true meaning and vital importance of the sequence—and the quadratos pattern that is its foundation—has remained hidden.

At its most succinct, the ancient sequence and pattern is:

I. *Gospel of Matthew:* written in Antioch in the 70s CE following the destruction of the Great Temple in Jerusalem. We experience the loss or ending of something dear or familiar. Initially frozen, we decide to move forward into the unknown, unexplored.

II. *Gospel of Mark:* written in Rome in the mid-60s CE during Nero's arrest and brutal execution of all believers in the Christ. As we move into the unknown and unfamiliar, we find ourselves bewildered, anxious and beset by struggle and conflict on all sides.

III. *Gospel of John:* written in Ephesus at the end of the first century in a time of harmony and abundant growth in the Christian community. Suddenly, something new arrives—a fresh concept, attitude, relationship, a way of life, an epiphany. This is often unexpected. And we find that we must simply *be*, rather than conceptualize or do, while we acclimate ourselves to the new.

IV. *Gospel of Luke:* written late in the first century from Antioch to the emerging Christian communities across the Mediterranean as Christians and Jews separated from each other and official Roman persecution began. We enter a time of gradual maturity as the new becomes familiar, learning its lessons, making them useful in everyday life and strengthening relationships in family and community.

This pattern is continual and concurrent throughout our lives. Just as one aspect of our lives feels "mature," another part will suffer a loss of the familiar. That will lead to another stepping out (Matthew), a new time of struggle (Mark), a fresh arrival of the new (John) and a patient time of learning how to make the new revelation ordinary and useful (Luke). It never stops. It only becomes deeper and richer—more so if we accept the process and join in with a full heart and spirit.

This is quadratos—the rhythm of God's breath that is at the heart of the gospel reading sequence and the center of a fulfilled life. It is the subject of Book One and Book Two. This book contains the fascinating history and overview of the ancient reading sequence of the four traditional gospels, and takes the reader through the first half of the quadratos journey, the Gospels of Matthew and Mark. Book Two carries the reader through the second half of the journey, the Gospels of John and Luke, and into a summary and challenge for contemporary Christianity.

It is my prayer that all of us will find our footprints within the circle of quadratos. Do I think you will leap to belief in my premise? No. But I hope you will read these books and think about quadratos. See if its logic appeals to your head and your heart. If it does, try some of these practices in your life. Observe how quadratos works. Test it. If it does for you what it has done for many, and for me—then pass it on to others. Because that means you will have found the vision and practice of your faith renewed, your relationships enlivened and, in general, the sense of purpose and equanimity in your life increased. That is the purpose of these books—just as it is, after all, the purpose of the gospels.

—*Alexander J. Shaia*
Christos Anesti!
Easter 2006
Santa Fe, New Mexico

BEYOND THE BIOGRAPHY OF JESUS:

THE JOURNEY OF QUADRATOS

BOOK I

ALEXANDER J. SHAIA

CHAPTER ONE

How Quadratos Was Rediscovered

Step-by-Step

WHEN I WAS seven years old, racists burned my grandmother's house to the ground. They waited for night to fall so they could slip through the shadows without being seen. First they scoured the house, digging in closets, opening up chests, stripping mantles of all her beloved mementos. Then they made a big pile of every Catholic artifact, crucifix, statue and family picture they had been able to find in her little home. Setting the crucifixes atop the heap, they poured on kerosene and lit their matches. Then they fled.

Fire engulfed the home in minutes. Summoned from my bed and rushing with my family from across town, I stood outside the house and watched, despairing, sure that my beloved "sitto" was inside, perishing in agony. After all, she walked with a crutch and could not have escaped. The fire was so intense we could not brave it to search for her. Hours later, Sitto appeared with a friend who had fortuitously taken her for a car ride that evening. Her restoration to us was joyful, but the roar of the flames and the smell of the charred wood I experienced that night had given me a visible face of hate; one I have never forgotten, nor wish to.

The fire happened decades ago in Birmingham, Alabama. Much has certainly changed since that time. But much in our world has not changed. Hate has not left human hearts. For me, the indelible lesson I learned from the flames was that the price of exclusion—of holding anyone as "outside"—is appallingly high. It is pain and terror and even loss of life itself.

In that 1950s Southern community, all of us in the Shaia family were certainly outsiders. My grandparents had emigrated from Lebanon, and we were Maronite Catholics. At that time, Birmingham was less than one-half of one percent Catholic, and Maronites were a tiny, obscure Catholic minority. I was truly a minority of a minority within an immigrant minority in a city that was not kind to minorities.

Nonetheless, despite the intolerance and misunderstanding that pervaded my early life, within the circle of my large Semitic family I had a childhood filled with beauty, mystery and love. "Semitic" describes the culture shared by the settled village people of Israel, Jordan and Lebanon, as distinguished from the nomadic Bedouin and Arab traditions. Even transplanted to America, our culture had changed little from that lived by my ancestors. My grandparents, aunts and uncles were as familiar to me as my parents, and my cousins felt like my brothers and sisters. Family and faith made up the cornerstones of our "village." We spent every Sunday together, usually at my grandmother's, and the rhythms of that day never changed: morning mass, shared breakfast, an elaborately prepared lunch, all followed by an afternoon of leisurely conversations, cards and sports. At nightfall, each family made its way home, knowing that the next Sunday and the next and the next would be the same.

The greatest treasures of my childhood were my "sitto," my mother's mother, and my "jiddo," my father's father. Both lived until I was in my late 20s and they were the heart of our family. I never heard Sitto speak an unkind word of another, not even after the fire. She was, and her memory still is, the anchor of compassion for me. Jiddo was a peddler and folk healer who was well known in our community. He explained he was forbidden by tradition from healing his own family, but I remember friends knocking on his back door. I can still see the focused and caring look on his face as he left to attend to them. He smelled of the earth and mystery and represented wisdom to me though he could neither read nor write. He was the first mystic I knew.

Sitto and Jiddo immersed me in the richness of their Middle-Eastern heritage, which was still their primary world, in many ways. Their daily life was filled with the word pictures painted by Arabic idioms, and their stories instilled in me a poetic heart. When I asked (often) for the English translation of an Arabic phrase, their patient reply was: "Oh, honey, Arabic is poetry. I cannot express it in English." But when I pressed, they would say, "Well, it's like this…or this…or maybe that." Beautiful words that made beautiful mental pictures, drawn from the language and traditions of centuries, came to fill me.

When I left this sheltered village and entered the University of Notre Dame, I suddenly found myself engulfed by a maze of philosophical discourse. Immense words and theories swirled around me, but they did not speak of my culture and the God I knew. The God I understood was founded in poetic mystery, not reason. Worship was an experience I could feel in my body, not an ideology. Confused and lonely, I felt I was an outsider.

I floundered in this new, complicated environment, and neither my early Maronite Catholic understandings nor the academic concepts I was studying sufficiently addressed the challenges I faced. I needed structure, but nothing I attempted seemed to work or feel comfortable. I began to look for alternatives, and found myself majoring in Cultural Anthropology with a focus on indigenous peoples and their rites of initiation. I found these traditions beautiful, closer to my own culture, and more adaptable to change than the western systems of thought on which I had been focused.

Within my anthropology studies, there was another pattern I noticed. Although each people I studied had their own cosmology and stories, their own vocabulary and worldview, each also described a four-stage journey of spirit that was deemed necessary for moving from childhood to adulthood. The first stage always called for "entering," and involved ignorance and loneliness. The second always held pitfalls or trickery. The third brought dawning understanding, even ecstasy; and the fourth held a process of transformation, which was carried back into the community in some way. Perhaps because they touched some sort of ground in my Semitic heart, these simple, yet arduous, steps held an emotional logic to which I responded deeply. The four-step process seemed to echo. Although I was not to understand why until many years later, it simply "made sense" to me.

Feeling more grounded, I was then able to find theology teachers who helped me connect the richly embroidered past of my heart, my anthropology studies and the intellectual abundance of western and Christian thought. In particular, Henri Nouwen, John Dunne and Morton Kelsey helped me to trust in the wisdom of my first culture and started me on a path toward resolving my conflicts. C.G. Jung and Joseph Campbell, both of whom largely wrote for westerners seeking their way back to a mythic life, helped me discover a bridge between the mythic (though unreflective) Lebanese tradition in which I had been raised and the post-modern western world in which I now lived. My time at Notre Dame set me searching for a rare balance—critical thought coupled with deep feeling, and new vistas made ordinary and practical.

Following Notre Dame, I entered seminary. Every Alexander— save three—in my family, since the year 1300, has been a Maronite Catholic priest. Clearly, this was also to have been my path. But when I reached seminary, I discovered that this long-anticipated home failed to nurture my spirit. Instead, I found a Church that was losing its deep resonance, and becoming narrow and lifeless. Though the decision rocked my entire world and filled me with the pain of a dying, ancestral tradition, I left seminary. This time, it was my own home that burned. My own decision had set the fire. And still I stood, outside, watching.

After leaving seminary, I joined the staff of a Catholic parish. At that time, the Roman Church was in the midst of dramatic changes. One of them was the restoration of the lengthy and ancient process of Christian baptism, which was much more extensive than the simple pouring of water. I was asked to help implement this change, and my duties became focused on this process and the spiritual renewal it promised. As I explored and worked with it, my anthropology studies allowed me to immediately see its profound links to other wisdom traditions I had studied. Here, in western language and culture, in a high Catholic ritual, was a four-fold rite of initiation and maturation, with the same grace, deep truth and power I had intuited in my Semitic culture and had also found when I studied the practices of indigenous peoples.

The Catholic Church has ornate names for the four steps of the full ancient baptism process (Inquiry, Catechumenate, Purification/Enlightenment, and Mystagogia). But these complicated words defined the same basic stages I had seen so often in indigenous cultures. As I facilitated the rite and taught about it in dioceses across America, I became more and more convinced of its wisdom and broad efficacy. I even wished its stages could somehow be in regular, ongoing church ritual, and not just the initiatory sequence of baptism. I started to wonder if the four-stage, or four-step, or four-path structure itself, that I kept finding in these apparently diverse transformative journeys, might be significant and, perhaps, hold its own truth.

Then, ten years after I graduated from Notre Dame, I entered a doctoral program in Clinical Psychology. Through those studies, I met and trained with Dora Kalff, a Swiss Jungian analyst, devout Christian and practitioner of Tibetan Buddhist meditation. She had combined a therapeutic technique known as "sandtray" with the principles of Jungian psychology and the meditational practices of Buddhism. Frau Kalff called her synthesis "Sandplay," and within it I saw the four paths once again —this time in a totally contemporary and cross-cultural setting, in the practice of psychology.

In Sandplay, one creates a scene or picture in a tray of sand by shaping the sand and (or) placing figures and objects in it. Over the course of making a series of these scenes, a personal narrative begins to unfold on a level beneath conscious awareness. Healing comes through the subconscious process of creating and "telling" the story.

When I began my clinical practice, I chose to use Sandplay as my primary therapeutic method and became a practitioner and certified teacher. I consulted on myriad cases throughout North America, as well as Europe and Asia. Over and over, I saw the same four-fold pattern sequentially disclosing itself. Sandplay psychotherapists often identify one of the earliest scenes made by clients as a *Numinous Tray* that holds images that indicate the intent to submit to an inner journey. This tray is followed by a series of scenes describing increasing tension, polarization and conflict. In the next phase a scene will appear that is called a *Self Tray*, which reflects an experience of Union. Eventually, a series of trays will show a return to everyday life, but with a larger sense of consciousness that includes obligations beyond the personal self.

As a practitioner, I have seen hundreds upon hundreds of Numinous Trays and Self Trays and the trays that followed them. It didn't matter if the clients were children, or women or men. It didn't matter if the figures they chose were icons from current culture, mythical figures or phantasmagorical creatures, nor if twigs or seashells or bright, glittery stones surrounded them. In every single instance, the outer story told matched the inner story experienced, and the pattern was invariably four-fold and sequential. This happened with or without the conscious intention, or even awareness, of the individual. To me, the conclusion seemed inescapable.

I began to wonder if anyone else had noticed the pattern. To start, I learned that in ancient literature, storytellers identify four parts in great myths and epics: Summons, Obstacles, Receiving the Boon and Return to Community. When I read *The Different Drum: Community-Making and Peace* by Dr. M. Scott Peck, I saw four stages of community formation, although described by a different vocabulary: pseudocommunity, chaos, emptiness and community. Then I read *Original Blessing* by the then-Catholic priest, Matthew Fox. Though the Roman Catholic Church found his writings controversial and ultimately unacceptable to them, *Original Blessing* announced four paths of religious progression, which Fox named Via Positiva, Via Negativa, Via Creativa and Via Transformativa. Next, I turned back to the classics of western spirituality, and in Theresa of Avila's *Interior Castles*, there was the same sequence—although she broke the pattern into seven houses or castles rather than four.

I looked beyond Christianity. My college studies had told me about the four-fold pattern in indigenous cultures, but I found it also in Judaism's pre-eminent story: escaping slavery in Egypt, wandering in the wilderness, arriving in the Promised Land and making the Promised Land their long-awaited home. And, although the vocabulary is quite different, the same sequence can be discovered in The Four Noble Truths of Buddhism. I found that Hinduism's epic accounts of Shiva and Vishnu likewise reflect the progression of four. At this point, I became absolutely certain that the four-fold journey was a universal spiritual truth whose imprint could be found across time, geography, culture and religious tradition.

Epiphany

I continued to practice and teach, never dreaming that what I was observing and learning would become this book, but suddenly, a decade later, in October of 2000, on a cold, star-filled night in Northern New Mexico, my entire world changed. I was on sabbatical, and had chosen New Mexico as an appropriately peaceful place. One evening, I found myself reading a recently published book entitled *The Four Witnesses*, authored by Robin Griffith-Jones, an Episcopal priest and Oxford University scholar.

It was through Jones' book that I learned how deeply and empathetically the authors Matthew, Mark, John and Luke had each written their gospels to specific communities of early Christians. As I read of the distinct nature of each long-ago audience—their historic, geographic and cultural differences—and how each wrestled with a unique and critical spiritual question, a sense of familiarity began to grow in me.

I paused. The four-fold spiritual journey appeared. I saw the faces of indigenous peoples growing into their communal lives. I saw initiates moving into the mature practice of their faiths. I saw troubled men, women and children moving figures in sand as they worked through trauma. Invariably, each face moved through four paths, and each path had the same emotional and spiritual challenge that was faced by a specific early Christian community. Suddenly, my enjoyment of the still night on the high plateau disappeared in the frenzy of my thoughts. The pattern of these same challenges, in this same progression, was all around me—in every instance I could think of. It was clear—and amazing.

Fortuitously, the retreat center at which I was staying had a Bible in every room. I grabbed one, turned to the Gospel of Matthew and started to read. I read through most of the night, accompanied by my illuminating new perspective. The import of the passages, the familiar words—that I had read hundreds of times before—transformed before my tired eyes. I noted that each gospel was organized around a different metaphorical landscape. Even the writing style of each writer seemed to synchronize with the message held by "its" gospel. These realizations awed and excited me. But a deeper revelation was still to come.

I suddenly remembered the ancient Sunday reading cycle, and how its non-chronological order had been a persistent theological puzzle to me for many years. The remembrance kept intruding as I read the gospels. I wondered again about its formation and purpose. Who had made it? Why? What was its truth? Was there possibly some significance to the fact that Matthew, Mark and Luke had clear storylines while John did not follow the usual progression but was written more as thematic meditations? Indeed there was.

For a long time afterward, I thought of what happened next as my "discovery." I now realize, that in fact, I discovered nothing. The deeper wisdom of the gospels found *me*. All of my upbringing and prayer and education and life experience had been preparation for the moment that came that night under the limitless stars. To me it seemed as though thunder sounded and a door flew open, though there wasn't a cloud in sight. I even think I know how Archimedes felt when he discovered the displacement of water and shouted, "Eureka!"

Suddenly and with perfect certainty, I understood the reason for the original reading cycle. I trembled in the dark as I saw revealed the landscapes of faith, the ancient journey that the early mothers and fathers had walked but which had been forgotten. I saw the four gospels as Christianity's great teaching of the universal journey.

Four early communities wrestled with *four* distinct sets of challenges when faced with *four* distinct sets of historical circumstances. There are *four* universal paths to spiritual maturity. There are *four* major levels to reach psychological maturity. The early Christian church placed the *four* gospels into a specific sequence. Without psychology, without all the self-knowledge we have gained in the last two millennia, clearly inspired by a much greater wisdom, those early fathers and mothers of Christianity managed to grasp and set out the universal progression in a clear and workable fashion. *The four gospels in ancient sequence disclose the full internal/eternal journey, the great and immutable design, the heart of God that moves all creation.* It has been there for us, all this time, leading us. In these, our most needful hours, it awaits our conscious rediscovery and calls us to a renewal of spirit by our fresh understanding and practice. For me, it has become this book, which I offer now to you.

To the book itself, I also offer a word—*quadratos.* Over the years, as I have worked my own way through the challenges of this new truth, I have found it helpful to have a concise and intuitive way to think about four-ness—a mental frame that could hold this new window through which I was trying to see. Arriving by grace, and newly minted, the word sounds almost-Greek, and pronounces four-ness, structure and organization to me. I have found it to be a helpful frame in which my mind and heart can readily hold, conceptualize and explore this rediscovery of the truth found in four.

Thirty years have now passed since I left the Semitic village of my childhood and experienced the heartrending collapse of my initial world. In that time, I earned degrees in cultural anthropology, education, religious education, pastoral counseling, a doctorate in clinical psychology, and a specialization in Sandplay psychotherapy. I have lived and taught in every region of the United States. I have worked in rural towns, suburbia and inner cities. I have served those with no formal education, as well as those in academe. I have faced and worked through the personal challenges of a maturing life and unfolding self in my historical, professional and personal families. My varied adult roles have included high school teacher, university professor, ritual leader, psychotherapist, spiritual director/guide, inspirational speaker, author, friend and struggling human.

I have received many gifts along the way, and I have tried to honor and nourish them, finding deeper treasures as I do so. I have in-sight. I know gratitude. I find wonder in each of my days. There are fires that still burn in my life, but most of them are the ones I start and tend at my Blue Door Retreat, in the high desert of New Mexico. Their flames are beautiful and warming, and I feel my links to the firewatchers in the eons before me.

Now, having written these books, I can see how I was guided, step-by-step, through the four-fold journey of *quadratos*. Learning the pattern of this journey has given me an inner peace in the midst of doubt and struggle. Today, I understand that every step and seeming mis-step has purpose and meaning. I know that I am inside God, I am with all people of all faiths, and not one of us can be cast out.

CHAPTER TWO

Preparing Ourselves for The Journey of Quadratos

Who Holds the Truth?

THERE IS AN immense dilemma in most spiritual traditions today—Judaism, Islam, Buddhism, Hinduism and Christianity. Many would even use stronger vocabulary and speak of crisis. The dilemma is one of belief, and of trust. Who or what holds the truth? Of course, there are those who do not feel, or share, this predicament. Some of us are perfectly happy and fulfilled believing that the specific words in the sacred texts we read are both literal and inerrant. Others of us have simply turned off—closed our minds and hearts to any form of religion whatsoever because we have been so injured or angered by the illogical or uncharitable practices of our faith. Then there is the group in which I include myself. We cherish our traditions and yearn for them to grow beyond their illogic and lack of charity—to become more like the embodiment of the great teachings of the faiths we follow.

Eminent scholars and pastors have dissected the traditional Christian texts, analyzing them, re-translating their words and searching out the history of Jesus in an attempt to answer the question of truth. Others have pored over newly unearthed documents and additional gospels in the hope of providing some lost message of Jesus, a revelation that would end all confusion. A huge industry has developed to feed our hope that the next fragment of papyrus or more precise etymological deconstruction will reveal something in which we can have faith. We have avidly followed the assertions of other writers—even of fiction—as they offered us findings they believe the early church suppressed for a malign purpose.

The differing answers we have received are not only confusing; they have effectively disqualified the traditional Gospels of Matthew, Mark, John and Luke. We have been trapped between head and heart. Are the four gospels found in the Christian Bible really there because they are genuinely more holy—spiritually truer or somehow more significant? That is what most of us want to believe. Or are they merely the four that survived for some now obscure reasons of power or privilege? Are there equal, maybe even greater, truths in the writings that have disappeared through chance or design?

With every new analysis, our hungry hearts plead with our minds, asking, "Who should be believed? Who can be trusted? What's the point of all this analysis? What we really want is the Great Design for our lives—the useful practices in Christianity that fully engage both our heads and our hearts. Where are they?" These have been my questions also. Book One and Book Two of the Journey of Quadratos—are my answer.

The Gospel Inconsistencies

As we go through these pages, you will see that I refer to Matthew, Mark, John and Luke as though they personally wrote down every word of the gospels that bear their names. In point of fact, many scholars now think it more likely that the gospels began as an oral tradition, and that each "author" represents words originally developed and taught aloud for many years.

In the case of each gospel, sometime during the first century CE, someone, or maybe a group—with full inspiration and deep compassion—crafted an entire body of teachings into a written document that was specifically refined to meet the needs of a particular community at a particular point in history. Perhaps this was indeed the "author." But maybe it was a scribe, or even a group of students. In early tradition, the Greek word *kata*, *"according to,"* was attached to each of the four gospels. It may have signified a kind of warranty that the gospels were "according to" the apostle, and the material in them was faithful to his accounts; or, it might have meant that the apostle actually transcribed the account himself.

What most people find more confusing than the question of actual authorship is the presence of significant discrepancies in the life of Jesus as recounted in the four traditional gospels. Careful readers know, for example, that the story of Jesus' birth varies dramatically in each account, and even disappears entirely in the Gospel of Mark. The Crucifixion and Resurrection accounts are equally disparate, as are many other details. Each gospel uses very different language, selectively highlights parts of Jesus' life and teachings, and employs a radically different metaphorical "landscape."

Some scholars argue that these discrepancies are nothing more than to-be-expected variations between eyewitnesses. This argument appeals to our hearts and is acceptable to the felt sense of mystery in these texts that goes beyond pure logic, but it leaves our heads puzzled. Other scholars, most recently Marcus Borg and John Dominic Crossan, contend that the discrepancies are crucial and prove that we cannot rely on the four gospels as an accurate account of Jesus. They wish to resolve the dilemma through historical research, searching for "truer" accounts of Jesus' life and the actual words he spoke. This premise appeals to our heads, and could give us historical accuracy, but little else.

Still other scholars, like Elaine Pagels, believe that the many writings from early Christianity are theological accounts, with little or no historical accuracy, that were composed by competing factions as the early Christians sought to define their beliefs. Eventually, some beliefs—and the writings supporting them—were accepted and others were rejected. This theory gives a pragmatic sense of how religion and social systems develop, but little else. The problem with each of these academic answers is that none of them really helps our questing hearts *and* minds. None of them is sufficient to resolve our sense of uncertainty, or our spiritual need. They neither completely defeat the gospels, nor do they bring their words—or the words of any other early writings—into manifest reality in our daily lives, emotionally, intellectually and spiritually.

Quadratos offers a starkly different answer—one that speaks to both head and heart. It is an ancient truth, and through it, we will come to understand that the discrepancies are not only correct, they are purposeful and useful. They derive from the way each gospel was composed. In the hundred years after Jesus' death, each of the four traditional gospels was written during unique historical circumstances for a specific group of early Christians in a distinct geographical location. In each case, the writer reframed the core story of Jesus' life, emphasizing, and even altering, its elements and giving each gospel clear relevance and guidance for the singular historical realities and dilemmas of its audience.

For example, Mark was the first gospel composed. It combined stylistic elements derived from the apostle Paul's earlier writings with stories shared by groups of desperate Messianic Jews condemned to death for their beliefs by the Emperor Nero in first century Rome. Those courageous believers would meet as they could in homes or cells and try to allay each other's fears and bolster their slim hopes through the ancient tradition of storytelling. As they did, their extreme emotional realities—their agony and their ecstasy—became folded into their recounting of the life and inspiration of Jesus the Christ. These stories combined present-moment realities with prophetic and instructive lessons. They were instructive, interesting—even exciting—and completely distinct from previous Jewish scriptures or Greco-Roman prose. They became known as gospels, meaning "good news," and they were a profound part of helping the community experience the Christ's continuing presence in their individual and communal struggles.

Mark then put this form into writing—he composed an official "gospel." His written story of the Christ was different from a lecture, or a formal sermon. Just as the oral form had done, Mark's stories enabled people to see themselves in the stories that were written down. When the stories were read aloud—or prayed as practice, which was their usual use in those early times—people listening could discern patterns and then understand that Jesus the Christ was not simply an historical figure, but an ongoing experience within each person, a doorway to the meaning and compassion and strength they needed to maintain their faith. This gospel form quickly found a home in Messianic hearts and took root. Later, Matthew, John and Luke all followed Mark's pattern of mixing stories of the historical Jesus with their communities' living participation with the Christ.

Perhaps it can be said that the long Jewish tradition of determination in the face of suffering kept the early believers from abandoning their young faith. While I am sure that fortitude was a significant factor, it does not account for the rapid spread of belief in the Christ, particularly in the face of great opposition. The ancient world was just beginning to discover the challenges brought by diversity, as tribes encountered each other. Perhaps the egalitarian and engaging gospel form was the fresh agent of communication capable of attracting them and carrying them onward through their dilemmas. I think it is likely that this new form of sacred story—so much closer to a conversation than a lecture or recounting of history—had a significant role in swelling the numbers of believers.

When Mark chose language and metaphors that would be meaningful to the Romans, in order to hearten them—and when Matthew and John and Luke did likewise, shaping many of the "facts" of the story they told—they did not betray the truth of the message of Jesus the Christ. To the contrary. Their inspired changes made that message real and alive to the people who needed it. The changes, the "discrepancies," made it possible for an early Christian community to live their daily lives with the sure knowledge that God was with them in their time of trial. Later, in the fourth century, those same discrepancies made it possible for the four gospels to serve the even greater purpose of quadratos. And today, those inconsistencies are re-opening that ancient journey again, this time for us.

The Ancient Mystery of the Gospel Sequence

In 315 CE, Emperor Constantine legalized Christianity. As Roman oppression lifted, and easy communication began to be established between the various Christian communities, Christians realized that wide differences in belief existed. Theological arguments erupted. Over the fourth century, various church councils were held, beliefs were standardized and practices developed, refined and formalized. One of the things standardized were gospels. There were many—at least fifty. Out of that number, the four gospels of Matthew, Mark, John and Luke were selected as the "true" gospels. Why only four gospel accounts and why these four? As noted in the Introduction, there are no written documents that definitively answer this question, but there are certainly abundant theories and some significant clues.

We know that Irenaeus, the Bishop of Lyons, attached divine and universal significance to the number four as early as 180 CE, insisting on "just four, no more and no less" because "natural and divine laws are quadriform." We know that early on, these four gospels in particular came to be regarded as four distinct accounts of one, single revelation and were entitled *Euaggelion*, which means "the good news of the kingdom." Eusebius, Bishop of Caesarea and a church historian, labeled Matthew, Mark, John and Luke "the holy quaternion of the Gospels" in about 300 CE.

Most importantly, in those early centuries, as disciples walked from village to village, of all the accounts available, it seems that these four gospels were the ones that were read to open new hearts. Believers chose to pray and pass these words on to others. The early communities appear to have found a power in these four gospels that was not present in other texts and, therefore, disseminated them more widely. It is my belief that their efficacy in the transformation of people's lives went hand in hand with the rapid and powerful spread of the Christian faith.

In the same general period that the four gospels were selected, they were also set into a specific reading order for Sunday services. The sequence was precise, and non-chronological. The words of each gospel were carefully separated into readings that were recited aloud every Sunday, on a designated date, in a three-year, repeating cycle. The Gospel of Matthew was read first in its entirety, followed by Mark, and then Luke. The Gospel of John was divided into parts that were read in the middle of each of the other three gospels and mainly linked to the Lent-Easter holy season. This reading cycle became the standard Sunday practice—in effect, the bedrock of the faith—for all Christian churches for over a thousand years.

How did this happen? Did the early Christians know of the ancient universal sequence that leads to spiritual maturity and did they discover it reflected in the four gospels as I have? Was this just some customary way the four were read? Were lots drawn? I do not pretend to know. It may have been happenstance or calculation, the work of an individual or a committee. My personal belief is that at the moment of discernment, the sequence of spiritual practices already known to work in human lives combined with the people making decisions and the circumstances of those decisions. A large helping of grace stirred the pot, and the pattern was set. I think it highly unlikely that we will ever be objectively sure. What we do know is that the reading cycle that was laid out in those early years held a great design and meaning that went far beyond the stories and lessons told by the individual gospels. And then the cycle was lost.

In the Middle Ages, the Church decided that it needed a simpler story. Few people could read, and the Christian Church was focused on solidifying Europe's feudal fiefdoms. In order to broadly spread a unified message, it was necessary to structure everything to be read aloud and quickly absorbed, and a short, straightforward telling became critical. The beautiful, complex three-year reading cycle—

which was a learning sequence and a process that required the recitation of all the passages of all four gospels—was abandoned. A one-year cycle replaced it: 52 lessons that told the major events in Jesus' life—a basic biography. Historically, it was an understandable change—inevitable, and perhaps even necessary—but the consequences for Christianity have been tragic.

Although the time-honored progression was still present in the rituals of baptism and the mass, when the three-year cycle disappeared, churchgoing Christians lost their opportunity to naturally and regularly discover and internalize an exalted journey. What had been the sounding of a great and resonant bell in the hearts of believers dwindled to a barely-heard whisper. The ancient pattern, though not totally absent, became indistinct and dim. Gradually, understandably and unfortunately, Christianity became focused on the details of Jesus' historical life—the least important part of the faith.

Subsequent centuries saw the rise of education, the invention of the printing press, the dissemination of books and the subsequent Protestant Reformation. The public began reading the scriptures; fresh translations appeared, and many Reformation congregations returned to reading the entirety of the four gospels at Sunday service. Unfortunately, none of the traditions seemed aware of the ancient three-year reading sequence. The great design had truly been lost.

More centuries passed. Suddenly, in the 1940s, the Roman Catholic Church, after hundreds of years of locking scholars out of the Vatican libraries, reversed course and opened its immense collection for research. The ancient three-year cycle was rediscovered. After much study, the Roman Church, seeing the cycle as a way to have all of the core gospels read, communicated and used for worship—and hoping to increase membership, but with no deeper purpose or understanding—reinstated the three-year cycle in the early 1970s. Within ten years, the Episcopal, Lutheran, Presbyterian, United Church of Christ and Methodist churches followed suit. Today these Christian churches, with minor exceptions, all read the same gospel passage on the same Sunday. *(See Appendix A for a schematic of the restored cycle.)*

Despite the reinstatement, however, no one in Christianity has ever offered any real explanation of the purpose of the original sequence—presumably because they have either forgotten it or never known it. In my experience speaking and conducting workshops for the last several years, the response I have had from church leaders when I explain quadratos to them has generally been surprise that they could have missed something so completely obvious—much as we all tend to overlook many complexities that are often concealed within our well-worn patterns and long-accustomed ways of thinking.

One of the frequent questions I am asked is why the reading cycle was set up as three, instead of four years—one year for each gospel. The simplest answer is that it takes three years to read aloud through all four gospels in small, manageable Sunday portions. A deeper answer is that three of the gospels, the ones called the "synoptics"—Matthew, Mark and Luke—have clear storylines, while the Gospel of John is less a story and more a series of thematic meditations. John's gospel—which appears largely in the Sunday cycle during the church seasons of Advent/Christmas and Lent/Easter—illuminates, deepens and completes the message of the other three gospels.

It is difficult for me not to be frustrated by the widespread belief among Christian leadership that both the original and current purpose of using the three-year Sunday reading cycle is because it is "a fuller reading" of Jesus' message. My background in psychology, anthropology and theology tells me the early Christians' careful division and sequencing of the gospels did not occur just to create "a fuller reading." While we may never know the precise reasoning behind the original formation of the sequence, I can, with absolute confidence, assert that it holds a profound spiritual logic—one that is universal, and also psychologically valid and precise. The four traditional Christian gospels in their ancient reading order reflect the truths of this universal four-fold progression—which I term quadratos. Furthermore, the inconsistencies in the gospels match the distinguishing characteristics of the truth held by each path of the sequence, demonstrating that the discrepancies are not only correct, they are purposeful.

Most Bible scholars today are blissfully engaged in the hunt for new papyrus, waxing when they read the beautiful words of Thomas' or Philip's gospel, finding perceived substance in the Gnostic texts, or busily excavating history as a vast intellectual treasure trove. But when those scholars read the gospels, I think they are looking for something different than I am. I am interested in the spiritual practices that transform human lives, each and every day. And in these four gospels in their ancient sequence—and only these four—I know I have found the internal/eternal map of transformation and the living treasure of the Christian faith.

The Great Map of Transformation

Whatever your vocabulary, whatever need you feel in your heart, whatever religious or philosophical question you have in your mind, a vital answer can be found in an understanding of the ancient gospel sequence. And the design has relevance for each and every one of us in the world today, no matter what our faith is—or even if we claim no faith at all. Following is a summary of the journey of quadratos, and how it is reflected and experienced in the ancient reading cycle of the four gospels:

The First Path, Climbing the Great Mountain, The Gospel of Matthew: Matthew's gospel was written to the Messianic Jews of Antioch two to five years after the destruction of the Great Temple of Jerusalem and all its priests. The Jewish community was being torn apart by intense grief and tremendous struggles. The Temple had represented the center of their lives, and they were certain that Yahweh (G-d) had abandoned them. They felt alone and frightened.

Matthew used the image of a mountain as a deeply poignant and evocative metaphor throughout his gospel because Mount Moriah, the site of Jerusalem's Temple, had been the holiest place in Judaism for millennia. He knew the power of this image for his fearful and faltering readers and he used it to bring the Messiahians to a new truth. Through it, he revealed a revolutionary teaching of Jesus the Christ to the Jews: they no longer needed a bleating lamb, a particular place, a physical temple, or even the mediation of priests as a condition of faith. Jesus taught of a new temple that was found within each individual and among all. And this new temple mandated full personal responsibility for the condition of one's heart and behavior.

In the first path of our own spiritual journey, we find ourselves in much the same place as the Jews of Antioch. We have been going about our lives in an unreflective way. Suddenly, we are brought up short by the crumbling of a part of our life we have taken for granted. Maybe a loved one dies, or our finances fail, or we are betrayed. Suddenly, all the habits and assumptions we've built up don't help. They fail us. We don't know what to do. We feel lost—lonely and estranged. Trying to find a solution, we whirl around in desperation, trying this, avoiding that. Finally, we take a small step out of our confused and self-involved spin and begin the journey. But we are immature and ignorant, and when we enter the unknown, inevitably, we fall short. We begin again.

The Second Path, Crossing the Stormy Sea, The Gospel of Mark: The Rome of Mark's gospel was a terrible place for the Messianic Jews. Made scapegoats by Nero and held responsible for an immense seven-day fire that had burned much of Rome, they found themselves at the mercy of the Centurions knocking on their doors searching for followers of Jesus. Once found, these believers and their entire family were taken away, horrifically tortured and murdered before crowds in the Circus Maximus. Jews faced death if they refused to inform on others. The entire Jewish community was in chaos, bitterness and despair; and the Messianic Jews were asking themselves if their belief was true, and was it worth the sacrifice of their lives and their children's lives? Mark's stark language and metaphorical images of wilderness and trackless sea reflected the bleakness of the Messiahians' dilemma.

21

Each of the messages Mark offered held both despair and hope. His account of Jesus' life and teachings assured the Roman Messianic Jews that their suffering—or even death—fulfilled a plan greater than their individual lives. He helped his listeners believe and trust that God had not and would not abandon them. He assured them that their time of suffering would eventually end. Even the lives lost, he told them, held value and meaning and would benefit future generations.

The second path requires great endurance. While most of us are probably not facing imminent physical death, we still quake at the strangeness of the new reality we have entered. It feels alien and filled with fear, but we can't turn around and go back, because we know the old ways won't work. Our ego-self, author of all our well-worn patterns of behavior and thinking, finds itself under assault. It desperately tries to re-establish control. Persistent, it sets up deceptions, which we must unmask and ignore if we are to continue on our journey. Competing voices and values tear at us. We feel lost, and are even afraid we might die. Somehow we remain on a course to a distant future, a place we cannot yet discern. The glimmers of hope and faith that we remember and find in prayer and meditation sustain us. We clutch them with grim determination.

The Third Path, Resting in the Glorious Garden, The Gospel of John: The Gospel of John stands apart from the other gospels in many ways. Rather than employing a storyline of Jesus' life to accomplish his objectives, John used long, philosophical narratives, with a primary metaphor of garden—and specifically that of the Garden of Eden. It is likely that these discourses were used as prayer—part of believers' preparations for the early Christian baptism ritual in the city of Ephesus. By the time this gospel was written at the end of the first century, followers of Jesus called themselves Christians, and came from many backgrounds, not just Judaism. The new faith spread rapidly in this thriving port city and spirits were high—but the euphoria of those high spirits threatened to slip into self-righteousness and division. John sought to establish a common and deeper grounding for the young followers of the Christian faith and warn them of the dangers presented by their immaturity.

When the Gospel of John was placed in the reading sequence, it was broken into parts and put in the midst of the recitation of each of the other three gospels. This placement tells me that if the Christians of the third and fourth century did in fact put the reading cycle together with conscious intention, they certainly knew the rigors of the spiritual journey well—and also had a terrific grounding in basic psychology. They knew that if the journey could be sustained, a moment of revelation would arrive, but that the wonderful moment was simultaneously glorious and dangerous. The seeker would receive an epiphany, but there was grave danger that he or she could quickly "lose it" or significantly misconstrue it. With the gospel placed in this fragmentary way, John's words are there throughout the journey—sounding a recurring and carefully calculated call of hope, promise and caution to weary souls under-going the challenges of living life and growing spiritually according to the teachings of Jesus the Christ.

There are other times in our lives, however, precisely as those early Christians anticipated, when the separated sections of John's meditations cohere into a revelatory whole—a complete, complex and glorious garden, an ecstatic, poetic song of the soul. After the tri-als represented by the Gospels of Matthew and Mark, the pieces of ourselves, the pieces of our lives and the pieces of the gospel—all the things that have seemed so separate—suddenly, and usually unex-pectedly, come together. Almost miraculously, everything makes sense. At these times, the full Gospel of John is nothing less than a life-giving oasis in what had seemed only an endless, trackless sea of sand.

When these moments arrive, we should rejoice, just like the Christians of Ephesus did. Exhausted from the agony and confusion we have endured, we want only to open to this wondrous and radiant experience. In us, all around us, the mystery of union unfolds and we feel, deeply, the truth of oneness with Spirit. We are filled with ecstasy, or perhaps the deepest calm we have ever known.

We want—and need—to stay awhile. We must hold to an inner stillness, reflect and allow the parts of us still mired in shame and unworthiness to come forward and join the divine embrace. Everything we see wears the face of love, as gratitude awakens and grows. Gradually, questions of obligation arise and we realize that our new truth has further responsibilities and that if we do not meet them, our revelation will sour into pain and division. Recognizing that we are still immature, that we have more to learn, we make the choice to leave this still unfinished—though blissful—state. We continue the internal/eternal journey.

The Fourth Path, Walking the Remembered Road, The Gospel of Luke: The Gospel of Luke was written as a two-volume document in the last part of the first century, intended to assist and instruct various communities of Christians throughout the Mediterranean region. Although growing and thriving in their faith, many Christians bore new pain, as they were formally cast out from Judaism, their mother faith. The Roman Empire also instituted more stringent legal sanctions against the practice of Christianity after the schism with Judaism in the mid-80s. These two historical events presented significant obstacles to the emerging Christian communities. How were they to respond to hurt? To oppression? Part of Luke's answer is contained in his primary metaphor. The first volume is concerned with Jesus and his disciples; the second volume with the apostles Peter and Paul. In both volumes, everything happens on the "road," or while traveling. The destination is secondary or unimportant.

Luke called the early Christians to practice. He asked them to change their previous ways of responding to difficulty and crisis, telling them to model their lives on the example set by Jesus and the apostles Peter and Paul. He encouraged them to offer compassion when faced with oppression and thereby demonstrate the values of

Christianity. He instructed them to trust in their spiritual practice, and have faith that the changes they sought would ultimately arrive. Luke asked Christians to forsake any bitterness over their separation from Judaism, and to avoid direct combat with the Romans. His narrative reiterated, over and over, that the only proper course for Christians was to "be" the change they desired.

In the fourth path, we are much like those early Christians. Our ego-selves have to become grounded. We have to learn the new behavior—not just theory—of a new way. Our inner guidance must mature, so that we may reduce, even eliminate, the old ego-self's protective and controlling reactions to events. This path of full psychological and spiritual transformation takes time. As it becomes familiar, we discover that the new way is more fluid and less predictable than the ways we have known. Our daily practice grows into a faithful and ongoing study of joy, compassion and integrity and our sense of equanimity strengthens. We come to understand that our journey will never end. The fourth path leads back to a new first path, filled with promise. As we reflect back and peer ahead, we comprehend this perpetual cycle of new beginnings and we welcome each fresh opportunity to learn and deepen in a conscious way.

It is this same four-fold sequence, I believe, that describes the process an artist uses to create—and a scientist uses to discover. It is the core pattern of all social, political and institutional change, as well as our civil discourse. We surrender, we struggle and endure, comprehension finally dawns, and then we gradually learn the practices that make our discovery, or our understanding, repeatable, consistent and real. I find it both humbling and inspiring to know that we walk to the same ebb and flow we hear in Mozart, read in Shakespeare and see in Michelangelo. This is the four-fold journey of quadratos, in its wholeness, and its universality. Whether we accept or decline the invitation to make it conscious, every one of us will be—indeed, already is—in submission to this monumental sequence.

This does not in any way mean that quadratos is precise or smooth or simple or linear. It is cyclical. In fact it is multi-cyclical. Questions arise in one path and begin to find resolution in the subsequent path just as they simultaneously yield to myriad new questions in another. We have and will travel each of the paths many times.

We will grow from the dependence of childhood to the autonomy of adulthood, sometimes alone and sometimes with company. We will be healthy and we will be sick. Life's seasons will constantly change and call out to us with their individual necessities. Different aspects of our lives will consistently appear at different points of the sequence. For instance, our personal life may be occupied with the challenges of one path, while our communal life is in another, and in the tumult of each of them, we may not even be able to discern our place in the sequence. Life, and the grace available to it, is rarely linear and well defined.

The journey is as complex as each of us. While most of us use our voice to speak, we also understand that the endless variations of tone and pitch make each of our voices unique. In the same way, our spiritual walk is both constant and infinitely variable, shared but at the same time singular. Throughout our journey, though, the underlying rhythm and pattern persist, and the rhythm beats in a measure of four.

Restoring the Ancient Pattern

The four-fold progression contained in the reading cycle not only predates most of the fixed structures of Christianity, but is also the foundation for many of its established rituals. The sequence is found in the design of the full baptism ritual—one of the most enduring celebrations of Christianity. The four elements of decision, prayer, illumination and commitment to service perfectly echo the lessons taught in the gospel order of Matthew, Mark, John and Luke. Scholars tell us that the full, four-step process leading to baptism had formally appeared by 300 CE. The gospel sequence and four-step process for baptism so perfectly mirror each other that I must conclude that the two grew together and became established in the same time period, sometime between 150 and 300 CE.

We also find the sequence in other aspects of Christian practice as it developed. Beginning in the fourth century, faithful Christians thought it their solemn duty to make a pilgrimage to Jerusalem once in their lifetimes. However, by the twelfth century, the journey to Jerusalem had become unsafe, and the labyrinth entered Christianity as its symbolic replacement. Both pilgrimage and labyrinth displayed a four-fold progression. First: the pilgrim makes the decision to set out on his journey, or to cross the labyrinth's threshold. Second: the pilgrim embarks on the journey, follows a circuitous path while paying careful attention and praying fervently. Third: upon arrival in the holy place, or center, the pilgrim spends time there, in reflection. Fourth, and last: the pilgrim returns home, back out through the pattern, with his prayers focused on integrating revelations gained back into everyday life. This is precisely the journey of quadratos.

The Catholic ritual known today as the mass (called *The Breaking and The Eucharist* in earlier western tradition) also reflects the sequence of four. First: the believer forms an intention and enters the sacred place (church) for mass, opening her heart to the inspiration and challenges revealed by the reading of scripture. Second: the homily, or sermon, charges her with stringent self-examination. Third: she experiences the union, the one-ness of All with God, called *communion*. Last: the believer receives the missa, (the literal meaning of which is "to be sent") made in the form of a blessing at the very end of the mass, commanding her to take her experience back out into the world, in service.

Though often not set in any formal sequence, an intuitive grasp of all four paths can also be read throughout a variety of mystical and spiritual Christian texts by writers as diverse and venerable as the Desert Fathers and Mothers, The Rule of Saint Benedict, and the writings of Saint Francis of Assisi. In the twelfth century, Hildegard of Bingen, in her *Book of Divine Works*, wrote about "progress" in terms of a specific cycle of four, which she also called "the very pulse of life." She wrote that progress begins with a time of "purging and purification," followed by "confrontation with temptuous impulses," then moving into "vigorous life and enchanting fragrance," and finally reaching "the ripeness of nature and the perspicacity of the increasingly alert and mature human being."

In *The Interior Castle*, written in the sixteenth century, Saint Teresa of Avila speaks directly and precisely about the sequence, though she elongates the four paths into seven castles. Of the seventh castle she writes: "Do you think that your deep humility, your self-sacrifice, your bountiful charity and commitment to being of service to all beings is meaningless? The fire of your love for God enkindles other souls. You awaken them through the living example of your own virtues. This is no small service. It is great service!" In the twentieth century, Henri Nouwen and Thomas Merton filled their writings with their personal progression through the four paths, though they are not so named, and throughout their lives, both were committed to using their spiritual maturity in witness to issues and needs in the larger human community.

So we may see that yes, the four-path sequence has endured, which is to be expected, since it is a universal pattern. But for centuries, we have walked the paths only dimly, and without conscious intention. As you read and explore quadratos further, and particularly see the pattern within the four gospels, I believe you will understand why it is so critical for us to reconstitute the full, four-path design. For too long, western religions—and more recently, psychology—have been centered on a three-step pattern. For example, mainline Christian theology and spiritual direction describe a progression of Purgation, Illumination and Union. Psychology uses Surrender (or commitment), Testing (or trial) and Illumination (or resolution). The implication in all three-step designs is that once you have "It"—Union or Illumination—all you have to do is maintain "It." This is not only mistaken, in our present world, it is a dangerous misconception.

Dramatic conversion stories and seemingly instantaneous changes are the result of three-step processes. Quadratos shows what happens after the dramatic change. The old habits, attitudes or behaviors sadly and inevitably return with a vengeance. Or, elaborate fantasy worlds are constructed and maintained. In either case, anything approaching genuine community becomes impossible, and an individual is generally in worse condition than before beginning the journey. As we move through Book One and clearly by the end of Book Two, we will know that only by the full completion of the third and fourth paths do we ensure that our journey engages the responsibilities of spiritual maturity and reaps true benefit for others as well as for ourselves.

Earlier spiritual traditions, closer to natural rhythms and less cerebrally focused, probably had something closer to a four-fold practice. I have observed this frequently in my anthropological studies of indigenous people—past and present—in the way they formed community and concluded their rites of initiation. This historical and existing indigenous wisdom is in part why I so strongly suspect the four-gospel reading sequence fell naturally into place in the third century. It "fit" the known human experience, although it is doubtful they analyzed or articulated it in any way as a life process.

It is likely that as curious scholars continue to research the first century and discover more about where and how the four gospels were composed, some of the historical information in this book will expand, change or even be overturned. Should that concern us or disqualify my thesis? I do not believe so. The basis for this book rests on the ancient *pattern* of quadratos, not on historical detail. That pattern, and the selection and ordering of the traditional four gospels in the reading cycle, has a universal spiritual logic that I find irrefutable. Quadratos is an internal and eternal truth, and I believe it is the bedrock that guarantees the spiritual truth of the gospels.

This great map has finally found its way back to us. But neither our scholars researching the texts, nor the people speaking their words in our churches, nor the people listening to them are aware of the truths held by the sequence. Yes, many churches now have the early Christians' three-year cycle of reading the four gospels and the words are recited, but they sound flat and passionless, unconnected to the lives of the people who strain to hear them. Even though most church leaders give every bit of energy they have to the effort, exhaustion overwhelms them. The Skeleton has been re-assembled. But all of us—leaders and congregants—need the robust, living body with blood coursing, full of vital, active cells. If, as you read, you find this meaningful, please speak of this to others. The rhythm of life is four: quadratos, quadratos, quadratos, quadratos... We all need the conscious awareness of the design. We need the map, this ancient truth—the bedrock and living treasure of our faith.

A Significant Last Note

It is almost time for us to move forward into our study of the gospels. First, however, we must restore another piece of early Christian belief that has been tragically flattened and left by the wayside over the centuries. I don't know exactly how it happened, but it was probably a natural outgrowth of the end of the three-year cycle and the ensuing focus on the human aspects of Jesus' life and the crucifixion.

Today, in much of Christian conversation, the underlying assumption seems to be that Jesus was born, lived, died, was resurrected and then somehow died again. The overwhelming emphasis on the crucifixion and "Jesus died for our sins," found in much of Christianity, misses the point that the Christ lives! Early Christians did not make this mistake. They avoided it because they always used the full sacred name of *Jesus the Christ*, and they lived the truth of this name in their spiritual practices.

The apostle Paul is the earliest known Christian writer. In the approximate years 45 to 60 CE, Paul wrote extensively and translated many concepts from their original Aramaic and Hebrew (which was spoken in Palestine) into Greek, the language of commerce most widely understood in the Mediterranean region. It is generally believed that Paul's writings predate the first of the four gospels by at least five years. When he wrote, Paul chose the Greek word "Christos," which meant "the anointed one," to replace the Hebrew/Aramaic word "Messiah," which had a corresponding definition.

Paul genuinely understood the greater import of Jesus' words and life. He knew that the names "Messiah" and "Christos" were both inadequate. Although "Christos" was important, and would carry a strong part of Hebrew history forward, he knew he had to do more in order to faithfully transmit Jesus' message. He therefore tried to build an understanding through everything he wrote that expanded the concept of "anointed one." Paul knew he had the responsibility to carry the greatest of messages, not just to Jews, but also to all peoples. His example and precepts influenced gospel writing, as well as all four of the gospel writers, although we will see Paul's direct impact most powerfully in the Gospel of John.

Paul wrote that the Christ was "the spiritual rock" from which Moses drank (1 Corinthians 10:2-4). He wrote that Moses "suffered abuse for the Christ" (Hebrews 11:26). He wrote that the Christ was *"the image of the invisible God, the firstborn of all creation; for in him all things in heaven and on earth were created, things visible and invisible, whether thrones or dominions or rulers or powers—all things have been created through him and for him. He himself is before all things, and in him all things hold together"* (Colossians 1: 15-17).

Paul's writings made it clear that he knew the Christ as an overarching, eternal, holy power without individual characteristics of any kind, existing in all dimensions, in time and completely outside of time. The Christ was present with Moses, long before Jesus' physical arrival on earth, for example. Paul knew and wrote of the Christ as an *eternal reality*, and Jesus as an individuated embodiment of that reality.

Although Paul had frequent disagreements with the other apostles who initially saw things in a more limited way, Paul's views eventually prevailed. By the time the four gospels were written, and throughout the early centuries of Christianity, the full and formal name used by all believers was three words long: Jesus the Christ. If anyone used a shortened version, it still held the unlimited and immutable reality of the full name. From Paul's sacred title, the new religion eventually would derive its name—*Christian*, instead of what might have been more likely—*Jesusian*.

The understanding with which Paul imbued this great title also helped to create a new, unparalleled form of telling Jesus' story. By the time the first gospel was written, in those horrendous days in Rome, Mark was not limited to an account of the biography of Jesus. In fact, Mark and the authors who came after him were mandated by the spiritual experience of the great name to recount Jesus the Christ as a living, present-moment reality in their communities, even though it was some thirty to seventy years after Jesus' death and resurrection. It is startling how many scholars have failed to note this fact. For readers in those early days, who knew and accepted and acknowledged the resurrection without hesitation, the words Jesus *the* Christ in the four gospels automatically made them present-moment realities instead of historical biographies.

In the second, third and fourth centuries, this experience of Christ as a living reality was essential to the ritual of baptism. Individuals joining the Christian community after having completed the full course of study and commitment that resulted in their baptism, emerged from the waters to hear the entire assembly cry their name followed either by "a Christ" or "in Christ." Christians knew that the Christ lived— and lived in them. A thousand years later, this had been lost, along with the full four-step process for baptism and the reading cycle.

The Great Journey Today

Early believers in Jesus the Christ were sometimes called "Followers of the Way." For them, walking a Christian life was not a static reality; it was a continually unfolding process. By accepting that earlier understanding of the full name now, which we must do if we are to make the Great Journey, we are invited to participate in Christhood, the dynamic, ongoing process of creation, of quadratos. We are—each and all—invited into the continual cycles of death and resurrection, where human concepts of time and space have no meaning. We can become full participants in an eternal reality that is in constant movement, fluid and growing.

When we look at the four gospels we will find, not one Jesus who lived briefly two millennia ago, but a universal Jesus, a presence of the eternal Christ, who shows us a different face of wisdom and compassion in each gospel, in each path of our journey. The prophets and saints of the past will walk at our sides. We are—each and all—invited to go beyond the biography of Jesus and use a two thousand year old map, the four-gospel journey. We, too, can become Followers of the Way. The Christ did not die, but lives, guiding us in wisdom, and in compassion. When we recover this understanding, on a personal and communal level, we can have calm assurance that we can meet today's unexpected dilemmas with sound discernment. We can have the courage to hear the text of the gospels in new ways, neither slavishly tied to a literal history nor at the beck and call of personal whim and desire.

If we truly understand the heart of these books, our conversations with each other will change. The wisdom of quadratos will open to us, and in response, our own hearts and lives will flower. We will engage in prayer and conversation with each other that focuses on our spiritual practice rather than on theological ideas. Our ability to be intentional as we make our life journeys will increase—as will our ability to honor all other great faiths and ways of making the journey. Our eyes will meet in a respectful gaze. It will be possible for us to live in peace.

This is necessary now, today, as we find ourselves in a world of increasing complexity and genuine danger. We need the maturity of a fully formed spiritual journey, and the wisdom of true elders who hold us and help us to live through anxiety and challenges. We need to pray that our faith leaders will take up this challenge; but more importantly, we need to take it up ourselves and become the people we need now, and our children will need soon.

The first half of the Journey of Quadratos awaits. Enter it with me now, and begin its first path—Climbing the Great Mountain of the Gospel of Matthew.

CHAPTER THREE

The First Path: Climbing the
Great Mountain of Matthew

Before you enter this terrain
there are a few things
you should know.

There is no entry fee,
but it will cost you plenty
to make this journey.

Pack a lunch. Lose your map.
Travel lightly. The weather
is unpredictable.

I am prone to sudden washouts,
to the startling crumbling of earth.
It's good to watch your step,
but what is underneath is strong
and you are welcome to settle there
to rest for the night
or stay for a season.

Be careful at dusk.
It's when the beasts come to the water,
and it's not that they would devour you,

but they are protective of their terrain
and will not easily yield.
I can tell you
they will never be utterly tamed,
but with choice morsels
and soothing words,
you may have them
eating from your hands.

If these warnings sound harsh, good;
this terrain is not
for the faint of heart
or for those who would travel
its contours crudely,
littering its landscape
and stripping its soil.

But I think you are made
of stronger stuff
and more tender,
that you already know
the lay of this land:
how its treasures will yield
to your searching fingers,
how its wellsprings will ease
your traveler's thirst,
how its brambles and thorns
will give way
to the waiting hidden garden
where grows the sweetest,
most exquisite fruit
waiting to be consumed.

—Jan L. Richardson

Starting Out: Trust and Courage

AS WE BEGIN our journey, you should know that each path we will study has, within it, its own sequence. And while our individual walk may vary in its specific chronology, no aspect can be ignored or evaded or avoided. All of them will be our experience, regardless of their sequence. The good news is that you have already accomplished the first phase—and probably the second—without even realizing it.

The first part is fundamental and very important, but it frequently goes unacknowledged. It is our place of beginning. All spiritual journeying begins with the unique and specific elements of an individual nature and a life that has been lived and experienced. Each of our personal stories, even if unreflective to this point, is integral to the process. It is the matrix from which we will be formed and the ground on which we will walk. Our singular selves, in this very moment, are the first part of the first path.

A feeling of estrangement and loneliness marks the second part of the path. This feeling will arise within us at some point, and sometimes at many points, in our lives. We may not clearly understand that this experience is signaling the opening of an inner rift, but we surely feel its tremors. As they rock us, they alert us to a disconnection between our interior and exterior lives—often extreme, and sometimes total. We may push these feelings away; dismiss them as minor and "only" related to a specific outward event—a disappointment or a loss. We may choose to ignore them. This may be a successful strategy for us, at least in the short term, and if they are indeed minor.

However, when the dislocations are more extreme, we will find them more difficult to set aside. Consciously, we may only be aware of the ways they manifest outwardly—broken relationships, abuse, depression and fear. Yet the deep pain these cause us provides the impetus for change. It begins to make us willing.

Once the seed of change has been planted, we have begun a journey of spirit, whether we know it or not. Although we may struggle in this part of the path for quite some time—changing partners or substances, reading the latest self-help book, withdrawing—eventually we will be called onward. We will discover that the time and effort we spent skirmishing amongst temporary "solutions" failed to truly solve anything. Without this experience, we would be unlikely to find ourselves sufficiently opened and able to hear the invitation to a genuine transformation in our lives.

The invitation is the third part of this path. It arrives in myriad ways, differently for each of us, but within it, we will be able to discern the inward hope of a greater and more productive possibility for our lives. A far vista appears, and its beauty beckons our soul.

Thanks to the pain in our past, we will also have a kind of despair-fueled sense of resignation—a willingness to make a reluctant, yet vital, admission: we are unable to "go it alone." In some kind of amazing spiritual alchemy, an internal decision mysteriously forms. These hopes combine with our personal history plus an extra component I identify as grace. The decision pronounces, "I will" to the call for journey. It also holds a kernel of belief that we can actually manage to reach that distant, beautiful place—even if we do not yet understand how.

So we set forth, and a little way into the first path, we quickly encounter the opening of the fourth part, which appears as increased challenges. Immaturity and ignorance lead us into missteps and, sometimes, increased difficulties. When these arrive, we know just enough to understand that a return to the old ways is not wise, but a clear course forward isn't apparent. Despite our initial resolve, we are filled with powerful longings to return to our old emotional home, no matter how cracked and crumbled it is. We try to bring old answers to the dilemma, but they are ineffective with our new problems. Inevitably, confused and squirming around, we betray the intention of the journey—and even this betrayal is a necessary step.

In our floundering we start to soften a bit and learn to employ a new, often awkward, self-compassion. We begin to identify the inner sources of our errors and slowly start to correct their influence on our actions. Each time we are able to do this, an inner confidence grows. Every new understanding merits self-congratulation. Our increasing self-knowledge enables us to continue despite frustration and to do so with conviction instead of resignation. This ability to restore our course is the fifth, critical and concluding part of the first path.

The first path may last for a very long time. It has substantial trial and error within it, and it will certainly reappear over and over again as we cycle through the quadratos process many times in our lives. We will grow to recognize its arrival, and sometimes it will go more smoothly for us. But in deep crisis, it can retain the full awkwardness and pain of when we knew and had experienced less than nothing—but this is the stumbling struggle of beginning.

Within the Gospel of Matthew, a profound guide awakens us to the hope and challenge of the first path of quadratos. Our exploration of Matthew's gospel will begin with a study of its historical context, which starts long ago with Jerusalem's Great Temple and its importance to the Jewish people of the first century. Then we will move on—to the words and counsel of the gospel itself.

Before we enter these ancient times, let us prepare some common ground. Although the outer lives of people in the first century and ours could not be more different, we certainly have our own temples today. Each of us has beliefs, aspects of our lives we regard as fundamental, on which we rely for our interior stability. They may be health or body or love, family or fortune. We derive joy and meaning from them. We think, we hope, that they will never change. When we look back on them, or tell their stories, our mental editing is very charitable—all seems simple and golden. Sometimes we inherit these temples. Sometimes we build them. We count on them. No matter what they are, we consider them central, solid and sacred. We yearn to make them secure and expend great effort in attempts to make them so. They have real roles in our lives—but we are sometimes forced to discover that they have no genuine permanence.

Across time and culture, people have felt a desire for permanence. In reflections of their desire, they have imbued physical landscapes—

particularly high mountains and standing rocks—with meaning. Mountains connote the eternal; represent basic and unchanging security. Governments and companies regularly use them as iconic images to instill confidence and faith—think of insurance companies, banks, and the Rock of Gibraltar. Spiritual traditions have built pyramids and stone circles, raised altars on cliffs, put their temples on rock, and incorporated the metaphor into their foundational theologies.

Nonetheless, at some point, even rocks crumble. All of us come to the experience of enormous loss. What we believed would stand forever, trembles and falls. Dark chasms and precipices appear with the suddenness and drama of a volcanic eruption. It is at this point that we find ourselves standing on the first path, barefoot and covered in ashes. This is where the millennia disappear. This is our common ground. Our hearts could as well be in first century Jerusalem.

Earliest Days: The Great Temple of Jerusalem

In the first century CE, the Temple of the Jewish people was in Jerusalem, high atop the pinnacle of Mount Moriah. This had been its sacred location for a thousand years, and a place of Jewish destiny for two thousand. The Temple was the religious, political and financial heart of the Jewish faith, of its traditions, and was even deemed central to life itself.

The high altar of the Temple was believed to stand on the precise place where Abraham, the father figure from whom all Jews (and Muslims and Christians) count their lineage, built the altar on which to sacrifice his precious son, Isaac. Abraham's willingness to make that immense and extraordinary sacrifice—though his hand was stilled from completing it—had secured the covenant between Yahweh (the Hebrew name for God) and the Jewish people. And by that covenant, they had come to understand themselves as "chosen."

A thousand years later, King David was led to that same mountain. There he built a great city that he named Jeru-shalom, place of peace, now Jerusalem. Moriah's peak—the site of Abraham's surrender to Yahweh's will—was designated as the location for the monumental (and sole) Temple for the Jewish people. Although David never built the edifice, his son, Solomon, fulfilled his father's dream, and completed the immense structure that became known as the First Temple (or Solomon's Temple), about 900 BCE.

Over the centuries that followed, the Jewish people came to clearly understand that Solomon's Temple and the sacrifices offered there were, quite literally, the things that guaranteed God's relationship with them. In the hour before dawn each day, the high priest prayed and solemnly poured the blood of a fresh-killed lamb over the high altar. His actions reaffirmed and re-secured Abraham's covenant, assuring all believers that the sun would rise that morning. The whole Jewish order of creation depended on that prayer of that high priest, standing at that altar, in the still hour before dawn of that day—and of each and every day. It was a deeply accepted belief that when the Messiah came in accordance with the prophecies, he would come to this exact spot, to the holy place of Abraham's and the high priest's sacrifice. And he would come as a direct result of the perfection and fidelity of the religious practices of the priests and the chosen people they led.

Then, in the sixth century BCE, the Babylonians overran Jerusalem, destroying large portions of the First Temple, capturing and removing the priestly class into exile. Undaunted, their beliefs and traditions secure, the Jews laid the stones anew and rebuilt the Temple a mere hundred years later. Though this building was built on Solomon's foundation, it was called the Second Temple.

A new and more hopeful reality began for the Jews when Alexander the Great conquered the region late in the fourth century BCE. Alexander allowed much greater freedom of religious practice. His relationship with the people of Abraham was so benevolent that in the first year of his reign, the Jews named all of their first-born sons Alexander, which brought that foreign name into the Semitic world.

However, the peaceful time of Alexander's empire did not last. Alexander died only seven years after conquering Palestine. His entire empire was soon divided amongst regional kings. The new rulers of Palestine were the Greco-Syrian kings. Although their early reigns continued Alexander's benevolence, as time passed, their successors imposed increasingly harsh restrictions on Jewish life and worship, and attitudes toward the Jews shifted dramatically.

Eventually, there was desecration. The Greco-Syrian kings raised statues to their gods on the high altar of the Second Temple and held athletic competitions in its sacred courtyards. Nonetheless, the Jewish people and their priests held fast to their pride and faith. They knew that the Temple's basic foundation had stood for a thousand years, despite all trials. They were certain it would continue to stand and forever provide the security and promise of Abraham's covenant. As a great and chosen people, they stood confidently against every onslaught. Their sense of security could not be shaken.

In the mid-second century BCE, the Maccabean brothers led a Jewish revolt and re-secured the Temple. It was rebuilt, ritually cleansed, and an eight-day Feast of Rededication (which Jews now celebrate as Chanukah) was held in 164 BCE. Within twenty years of the reclaiming of the Temple, an independent Jewish state was completely in place, and the chosen people were once more free to live fully in their traditions. But the surcease was brief.

In 63 BCE, Syria and Palestine were absorbed into the Roman Empire and with the new government, a brutal occupation began. The people were heavily taxed, nearly to starvation. Rome ignored, even mocked, the independence of the Jewish people, and installed a single Roman candidate as both high priest and ethnarch (provincial king) over the region. Although the Jewish resistance and outcry against this step caused the two positions of priest and ethnarch to be separated once again, Rome persisted in its unceasing political pressure. The critical roles of both king and high priest became virtual puppet positions of the Empire, and were filled only by those who accepted Roman influence.

The Jewish people remained undaunted. Though small in number and resources, they firmly continued to believe they could throw off the Roman Emperor as their forbears had thrown off Pharaoh more than a thousand years before. Their views of their own power and destiny were unambiguous and frequently claimed. The Roman governor watched the community with a wary eye, and at each Passover, the springtime remembrance of the Jewish liberation from Egypt, the Roman governor became very, very nervous. As a huge and fervent throng came to make their annual sacrifice at the Temple, tensions inevitably rose.

Approximately ten years before Jesus' birth, there were actual riots during Passover. The Jews took back control of Jerusalem and held it for fifty days, until the feast of Shavuot, the celebration of Moses hearing Yahweh's voice on Mount Sinai (commemorated on the 50th Day after Passover). On that fiftieth day, Rome sent in its centurions. Although the outcome was in question for a while, Rome ultimately prevailed, and secured Jerusalem for itself again. However, thousands of pilgrims and hundreds of Roman soldiers died in the process.

Though re-conquered, the Jewish community spent the next six decades completing a major expansion of the Second Temple with undiminished zeal and determination. This was done despite Rome's brutal occupation—maybe even because of it. King Herod—who was half-Jewish—led the construction in an attempt to win the Jewish people's affection, and the expanded Second Temple, completed about the year 50 CE, was thereafter called Herod's Temple. This Temple was the architectural jewel of the eastern Mediterranean, and its magnificence beamed from atop Jerusalem. Once again, the Temple was the repository of Jewish faith and hope. Certainty about the permanence of this final temple was widespread, as was an increasing belief that the Jewish Messiah would soon come. Fueled by pride, long-burning resentments against Roman rule increased and smoldered, occasionally breaking out in violence.

By the year 60 CE, small Jewish uprisings had increased and over the next decade, fighting broke out across Palestine. A full-scale revolt appeared imminent. In 70, as tensions boiled, the newly elected Roman Emperor, Vespasian, decided to permanently deal with what he characterized as this "mettlesome band of thugs." Not satisfied to merely add to the Jewish body count and determined to completely and finally destroy the Jewish power base, Vespasian prepared the most devastating blow possible.

On the precise anniversary of the date Babylon destroyed Solomon's Great Temple, the Roman guard—under the command of General Titus, Vespasian's son—arrived in full and terrifying force. The massed troops marched in disciplined and thundering cadence to Herod's Second Temple, the center of Jewish life, and undertook to level it completely. There is no equivalent to what Rome did that day. The Temple's high altar—the center of worship—was shattered into tiny pieces. While some troops took down the massive walls, stone by stone, and removed them from the city, others burned all of the Torahs and scrolls and destroyed the holy vessels.

This time, Rome wanted no ambiguity and no contentious survivors in priestly exile. Titus' men massacred all of the Temple authority, the priests, the scribes, their families and tribal members. They slaughtered tens of thousands of Jews. Emperor Vespasian wanted absolute certainty that not one scrap of scroll, no tiny vestige of the Temple remained. There would be nothing at all left upon which the proud Jewish people could pin their hopes.

Much of Jerusalem was ransacked that day, but the Temple was a different matter. The soldiers' instructions were specific and crystal clear. No looting of the Temple was permitted; only its total annihilation. The guards followed their orders. When they were finished, nothing more than a flat platform and a bereft community remained. Vespasian's horrifying and decisive action accomplished its goal. The Temple, all of its authorities, and all of its worship had ceased to exist.

Even the earlier fall of the First Temple had not fractured Jewish faith as did this second and total destruction. When the Temple fell and its priests disappeared, the foundation of Hebrew cosmology shook. Judaism itself, leaderless, was in great danger. Somehow, everything the Temple had represented in the hearts and spirit of its people had to be rebuilt if Judaism was to survive. A re-birth was necessary.

Birthplace of the Gospel of Matthew:
Great Antioch on the Orontes, 70s First Century

After the massacre, the few remaining priests and Temple leaders fled to the city of Antioch on the Orontes, which resulted in that city quickly becoming the new Jewish center, one that was preoccupied with great challenges. There, in a time of complete chaos for the Jewish world, the apostle Matthew was inspired to write his gospel.

Antioch, Alexandria and Rome were the three great centers of the Greco-Roman world. Antioch was only a hundred miles due north of Jerusalem. Although there were several cities named Antioch throughout Asia Minor, Matthew's Antioch stood on the banks of the Orontes River, and was called Great Antioch. The Orontes opened to the Mediterranean Sea, providing a sheltered deep-sea port and a strategic location for Rome's regional military control. If we look at a contemporary map, the Orontes is known today as the Asi River and the Turkish city of Antakya lies over the remains of Great Antioch.

In the year 70, only nearby Jerusalem exceeded Antioch's Jewish population. The city's synagogue was grand and had special status, because it contained items that had originally been in Solomon's Temple (the First Temple), secreted away to Antioch when the Babylonians pillaged the Great Temple. Prideful worshipers, perhaps presumptuously, even referred to Antioch's synagogue as a "Second Temple." Additionally, Antioch's large base of Jewish leaders included many descendants of priests and Temple authorities who had fled there after the unsuccessful Passover-to-Shavuot uprising some eighty years earlier.

This city was a natural crucible in which Judaism could begin to reorganize and recast itself. Reform efforts began in the chaos of a bitter factional struggle that raged throughout the faith. Four factions arose and fought for the heart of the Jewish community.

One segment believed all hope was lost and was certain that an apocalyptic end time had arrived. They maintained that the destruction of the world—either by flood or fire—was imminent, and that the Temple's destruction had been the first sign of the final days.

The Pharisees, lower-level teachers who had risen to greater power when the priests and scribes were slaughtered in Jerusalem, headed a second group. They maintained that the Great Temple's destruction had resulted from God's wrath, brought on by laxity of religious observance. They therefore sought to unify Judaism through diligent observance of Mosaic Law and ritual practice, and maintained that it was only through this practice that the Temple would be restored and welcome the coming of the promised Jewish Messiah.

Another faction, perhaps numerically the largest one, was confused, unsure of what to believe or which way to turn. Many of these people simply wanted to get on with their lives. Others among them were fearful of any course, and waited for the "right" answer to appear—one that would provide them with a sense of stability and safety.

The final contingent was the Messianic Jews. The members of this group were extremely vociferous and very determined, though small in number. They saw both their context and their challenge as starkly different from the other factions. They believed that their Messiah had already come, and that Jesus was that Messiah. Their challenge lay in understanding what the Messiah expected of them in the wake of the loss of the Temple and their accustomed rituals, and in navigating the complications of the majority of the Jewish community who did not share their beliefs.

Today, we recognize this group as the early Christians, and they were Matthew's intended audience. He wrote his gospel specifically for them in their time of chaos, trial and difficult beginnings. Matthew wanted them to understand that their Messiah who had come, Jesus the Christ, taught that they did not need to mourn the loss of the Great Temple. The Temple of which their Messiah taught—the new Temple—stood within the heart of each follower, as a direct and personal relationship with God, supported by a community of like believers. It did not require a huge edifice or a special location. Matthew's inspired gospel became the prayer and practice of the Messianic Jews, and formed their spiritual foundation.

⸙

Approaching Matthew Today: Facing the Mountain

Matthew's gospel was placed first in the ancient reading cycle by the Christian church, even though it was chronologically the second gospel written (following that of Mark). When they placed Matthew first, they succeeded in offering it to all readers to use in the same way it was used by that early community in Great Antioch.

The Gospel of Matthew is a gospel of endings and new beginnings. It offered the Messianic Jews a message of hope and fresh promise. It offers the same to us. It is the gospel that most clearly conveys an understanding of the first spiritual path of quadratos. His metaphoric mountain and rock perfectly describe our own landscape in this first phase. As we make our way up our own mountains, we trip over pebbles, jump over rocks and try to climb over the boulders of our behavior, preconceptions and fears. How often do we stubbornly continue to believe in their permanence and solidity, even as we watch them shift and crumble, both from their essential instability and in the face of our persistence?

The patterns of Matthew's lessons are as inexorable as the lessons we must learn in the first path. They circle back over and over again, each building on the previous lesson, building to his inevitable, unavoidable conclusion. As we study his gospel sequentially, we'll see how his writing specifically addresses the first path, using every segment of Jesus' life to direct us to the development of our own inner resources, most particularly those of self-compassion and courage in the face of loss, and trust in the divine.

Fallible Icons: The Genealogy

The opening chapter of Matthew's gospel offers inspiration and reassurances, principally provided by the lengthy recounting of the genealogy of Jesus the Messiah. No other gospel has this recitation. Luke has a genealogy, but it is much less prominent and contains different names. Matthew's choice to start out in this manner accomplished a dual purpose for the Messianic Jews of Antioch. He holds up the entire line of names, allowing them to roll sonorously off the page in a majestic procession of historical Jewish icons. This told the Antiochians that they came from a great and long line of people who had suffered great loss, but who had prevailed. It reminded the Antiochians that they were descended from Abraham who had directly covenanted with God, and that they had inherited the warrior might of King David. They too were special, and they too were strong. This function of the recitation is explicit—clear to us even today.

Also explicit to the Messianic Jews was the clear recounting of the losses, betrayals, and twists and turns contained in the list. This told them to expect the unexpected, but not to be overcome by fear. It reassured them that their forebears had not only survived, but also discovered treasure in their reverses and thrived. Indeed, a further message emphasized that challenging traditional structure, rather than maintaining it, can bring great honor. This profound counsel and deep affirmation for the Messiahians came at a time when they found themselves unwelcome and disrespected by their more traditional Jewish counterparts.

The genealogy's implicit stories are less obvious to a present-day reader. Some of us may recognize the names, but generally associate them with the pinnacles those icons reached by the end of their successful life journeys. But Matthew's audience knew the entire stories—successes and failures—of these real, struggling human beings. Chronicles of Jewish heroes and heroines comprised the glorious heritage repeated regularly in their lives. They had grown up knowing the full drama of each person named.

There is no way we can replicate the quality of knowing that comes from oft-repeated stories learned from birth. However, I have selected a few stories and fleshed them out from information that can be found in the Hebrew Scriptures. As we go through the genealogy, we'll see how the icons become human, beset by woes, and fallible, just like us. This lets us absorb Matthew's message with an understanding that more closely approximates that held by the Messianic Jews.

Matthew's first line, a summary sentence, goes straight to the heart of the entire recitation. It begins with the central belief that Jesus is the Jewish Messiah, and immediately moves on to combine his name with those of the greatest of the great leaders, David and Abraham. To Matthew's original listeners, these words intoned: "This is your heritage; this is your belief, and this is the core of its truth."

An account of the genealogy of Jesus the Messiah, the Son of David, the son of Abraham... (1:1)

Matthew's lineage recites the direct line of Abraham: to Isaac, one of his sons, then to Jacob, Isaac's son, and then to Judah, one of Jacob's sons and methodically on, clear to Solomon, and eventually to Joseph, husband of Mary, who was the mother of Jesus. What can we learn from this genealogy?

Following early tribal tradition, Abraham had two wives, Sarah and Hagar. Hagar had a son, Ishmael, but Sarah was sadly barren until very late in her life. Then an angel appeared and told Abraham that Sarah would conceive. While she would have gloried in this news earlier in her life, at her advanced age, the prospect seemed so ridiculous that she laughed when she heard about the angel's prophecy. Nonetheless, her son, Isaac, was born. After his birth, ill will between the wives began and grew to such a degree that Abraham, at Sarah's insistence, cast out Hagar and Ishmael. Ishmael later became the patriarch of Islam. Abraham's choice flew in the face of tribal tradition, which clearly held that the birth of a son was a concrete sign of God's blessing, just as the lack of a son was a curse.

The human dilemmas in this story are huge. Sarah, miserable and "cursed" with barrenness most of her life had to contend with an infant as an old woman. Abraham had a houseful of angry, fighting women, and had to throw one of them out, along with a blessed son! Together, Abraham and Sarah, while completely settled in their life in Ur, subsequently found themselves forced into leaving everything they knew and moving to Palestine, a land completely alien to them. Their human lives were filled with unanticipated losses, predicaments and change.

The lineage continues with more elements considered highly nontraditional in their time. According to ancient tribal custom, eldest sons always inherited, and younger sons frequently received little or nothing, yet the list Matthew recited did not contain a single eldest son. Not one eldest son was chosen to continue the line of the Messiah that proceeded directly from Abraham, the patriarch of Judaism who had made the covenant with Yahweh! Abraham completely broke with custom when he made Isaac his inheritor instead of Ishmael, his eldest son. Jacob, the second son of Isaac, tricked his way into his inheritance in place of Esau, his elder brother. In turn, Jacob named his fourth son Judah as heir, bypassing three older sons and again deviating from the community's beliefs and expectations.

...Abraham was the father of Isaac, and Isaac the father of Jacob and Jacob the father of Judah, and Judah's brothers... (1:2)

Judah had three sons: Er, Onan and Shela. Although Er and Onan married, they were killed before either of their wives bore children. Judah, attempting to lift the curse of (male) childlessness from his family, ordered Tamar, Er's widow, to stay unmarried until Judah's youngest son, Shela, was old enough to marry her. Tamar acquiesced, but when Shela matured, Judah reneged. Tamar, needing children (preferably sons) to provide for her in her old age, took action. She veiled herself, and in disguise, seduced Judah. Being smart and prudent, she also persuaded Judah to give her his signet (seal) and staff before he lay with her. When she became pregnant, Judah sentenced her to death for the shame she had brought on his name through her promiscuity. When Tamar proved Judah's fatherhood with the signet and staff, Judah revoked his sentence and welcomed her back. She bore him twin sons, Perez (the elder) and Zerah.

...and Judah the father of Perez and Zerah by Tamar... (1:3)

Matthew's "calling of the roll" moves through many brave and iconoclastic men and woman and eventually gets to King David, his wife Bathsheba, and Solomon, a story that all Jews of the time knew very well indeed. They were rightfully and immensely proud of David, even though he had significant human flaws and a life rife with betrayals. After all, he built their holy city Jerusalem, united and expanded the Promised Land and ruled benevolently. Indeed, Matthew's wording specifically identifies David as an adulterer (he fathered Solomon "by the wife of Uriah"). David's shame, however, went far beyond the betrayal of marriage vows. King David slept with Bathsheba, Uriah's wife, impregnating her, while Uriah gallantly fought one of David's wars. Worse, he tried unsuccessfully to deceive his faithful servant Uriah about the paternity of the child, and when the deception failed, he sent Uriah back to the heart of the battle in a move tantamount to murder. Worse still, his hope that Uriah would die on the battlefield came true.

With Uriah's death, David married Bathsheba, only to have their child die as well, a sure sign that God had cursed them. David, in his old age, passed over his eldest son (by a prior wife) and chose his second child Solomon to inherit his throne. Solomon became the Jewish icon who represented wisdom, and to him fell the honor of building the Great Temple.

...and David was the father of Solomon by the wife of Uriah. (1:6)

The genealogy was a wonderfully wise and compassionate opening for the Messianic Jews of Antioch. With the rhythms of a chant, it speaks a proud and ancient history and brings it forward into a hopeful future. Though most of the names seem foreign to our eyes, to the eyes, ears and hearts of Matthew's audience, the litany must have seemed like the rising of a giant army of affirming angels carrying a message even more potent than a procession of glorious names.

The foregoing scarcely reads like the stories of a devout and holy people who lived circumspect lives of perfection, humility and generosity. These were imperfect humans, and their very imperfection was often the source of their heroism and their reputation. They had been tested. Their lives twisted and turned and they had suffered great periods of loneliness and estrangement. They knew confusion and conflict. They too suffered, experiencing the same feelings as the Antiochian Jews. Yet these heroic figures endured and their path of trial led directly to the coming of the Jewish Messiah.

Matthew's genealogy completely departs from the Pharisaic Jews' belief that the Messiah would come only from perfection, a blessing from God for perfect behavior and perfect religious practice. More than anything else, the genealogy affirmed the Messianic Jews in their great lineage, and inspired them to eschew the beliefs and customs of other Jews at that time who where caught in a legalistic, perfectionist notion of the Messiah.

So many of the lessons of Matthew's genealogy are ours, too , on the first path. Remember the beginning of this chapter? We each start with a history—a particular matrix that is only, and individually, our own. This is the hard ground on which we stand, facing the mountain rising before us. We have, however, an inheritance greater than just ourselves. We each have prophets and warriors in our past, people of great depth and endurance and spirit.

We are following in the footsteps of the daughters and sons of our own Davids, our own Abrahams. As we begin our journey, we will be wise if we take the time to identify these significant people in our history. We need to establish our heroes and heroines, our inspirational figures. We may be able to find them within our direct lineage, or we may discover a kinship further afield in our human family. In either case, what we are looking for are real humans whose frailties, challenges and successes have relevance to our own.

As we continue, throughout our full journey, but particularly during the stumbles of the first path, we will likely want to revisit, and even expand, the search for our "personal genealogy." We will learn more about ourselves, and as we do, we will discover better what heroes and heroines we need. Will we need the fortitude of Sarah, the careful prudence of Tamar, the self-forgiveness of David, the wisdom of Solomon? Or the practical nature of our grandmother? Or Nelson Mandela's unfailing ability to smile?

Receiving the Call: The Announcement of Jesus' Birth

Matthew concludes the genealogy with the story of Joseph, and clearly shows that the historical line of the Messiah came through Joseph, even though he was not Jesus' biological father.

...and Jacob the father of Joseph, the husband of Mary, of whom Jesus was born, who is called the Messiah. (1:16)

Matthew is telling a story of faith, and of faith tested—not a biography of Jesus. So his focus is on Joseph, a man who found himself with a great dilemma. Betrothed to Mary, which by Judaic law meant that they were married but not yet living together, he learned that Mary was pregnant. Joseph was devout, prayed regularly, tried to help others and followed all the rules. He was considered "righteous." He knew, when he learned of Mary's pregnancy, that the child could not possibly be his. He felt betrayed and trapped. His mind certainly swirled with questions and protests and we can be sure he began an internal search. Why had this pain come to him? Had he committed some terrible wrong to be so punished?

Joseph's predicament was more than personal. Semitic life demanded adherence to accepted custom. Villages were governed by social approval, and neighborly gossip was the arm of correction. If a couple argued at the breakfast table, the village knew every word and gesture by lunchtime. The small, tight society had clear expectations of behavior and response. Deviation caused shunning by the entire village, a fate genuinely worse than death, especially because the shame would forever taint the family name and lineage.

Descended from David, and, by extension linked to the Messiah, Joseph bore an even greater responsibility to the community. Should he risk ruining his family name by continuing the charade of his upcoming marriage, to a now-pregnant woman? Should he cast out the woman who had betrayed him? While neither option offered a painless solution, Joseph initially gave into tradition, and quietly asked Mary to leave.

Now the birth of Jesus the Messiah took place in this way. When his mother Mary had been engaged to Joseph, but before they lived together, she was found to be with child from the Holy Spirit. Her husband Joseph, being a righteous man and unwilling to expose her to public disgrace, planned to dismiss her quietly. (1:18-19)

History indicates that as a conventional and "righteous" man, Joseph unreflectively lived the life expected by his society, until the night he received a message from an "angel...in a dream."

Undoubtedly, as he received these divine instructions to complete his marriage commitment and welcome the coming child he knew was not his, he felt everything he knew of the world collapse.

Yet, Joseph faithfully complied, and in doing so, became a powerful exemplar of courage and trust in Matthew's gospel. Antioch needed this example of acceptance, which said: "Stay open to the inner messages of God. The feelings that may arise within you that contradict those messages—your assumptions and fears—are unimportant. So are the demands of your people and their traditions. If God asks you to, you must be willing to move forward, no matter what the cost."

But just when he had resolved to do this, an angel of the Lord appeared to him in a dream and said, "Joseph, son of David, do not be afraid to take Mary as your wife, for the child conceived in her is from the Holy Spirit. She will bear a son, and you are to name him Jesus, for he will save his people from their sins." All this took place to fulfill what had been spoken by the Lord through the prophet: "Look, the virgin shall conceive and bear a son, and they shall name him Emmanuel," which means, "God is with us." When Joseph awoke from sleep, he did as the angel of the Lord commanded him; he took her as his wife, but had no marital relations with her until she had borne a son; and he named him Jesus. (1:20-25)

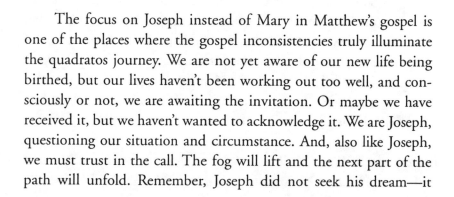

The focus on Joseph instead of Mary in Matthew's gospel is one of the places where the gospel inconsistencies truly illuminate the quadratos journey. We are not yet aware of our new life being birthed, but our lives haven't been working out too well, and consciously or not, we are awaiting the invitation. Or maybe we have received it, but we haven't wanted to acknowledge it. We are Joseph, questioning our situation and circumstance. And, also like Joseph, we must trust in the call. The fog will lift and the next part of the path will unfold. Remember, Joseph did not seek his dream—it sought him—and only with a similar calm and stillness can we discover the holy condition of our own journey.

It takes time to learn these new ways. Our experience is limited, and it may prove inadequate to generate genuine conviction. When we encounter doubt and anxiety, we can muster up those heroes and heroines for support as we grasp for solid footing. We can call friends who are further ahead on the journey. We can read this gospel, over and over again if needed. And we can pray. Matthew reminds us through Joseph that "God is with us! God is with me."

Homeward Star: The Nativity of Jesus the Christ

Matthew next tells the story of Jesus' birth. The account opens with the name of King Herod—historically a very dangerous figure—and then goes on to the sighting of a new star and the tale of "magi," wise ones, coming from the East. Signifying the rising of the sun and the direction the priests faced for morning sacrifice, East represented the direction of new beginnings, of hope arising in the face of darkness. There was also a Greek belief of the time that all people received the gift of a star at birth that served as a guiding spirit, similar to many people's trust today that each of us has a guardian angel or spirit surrounding us.

Consumed by fear over the threat of this new and unknown element, the Messiah, Matthew says that King Herod asked his scribes and priests where the Messiah was to be born. Using a subterfuge of false welcome, Herod relays the information to the magi, asking them to go and find the child and report back the location. The magi leave King Herod "and there, ahead of them, went the star" in the night sky, leading them directly to the newborn Jesus.

In the time of King Herod, after Jesus was born in Bethlehem of Judea, wise men from the East came to Jerusalem, asking, "Where is the child who has been born king of the Jews? For we observed his star at its rising, and have come to pay him homage." When King Herod heard this, he was frightened, and all Jerusalem with him; and calling together all the chief priests and scribes of the people, he inquired of them where the Messiah was to be born. They told him, "In Bethlehem of Judea; for so it has been written by the prophet: 'And you, Bethlehem, in the land of Judah, are by no means least among the rulers of Judah; for from you shall come a ruler who is to shepherd my people Israel.'" Then Herod secretly called for the wise men and learned from them the exact time when the star had appeared. Then he sent them to Bethlehem, saying, "Go and search diligently for the child; and when you have found him, bring me word so that I may also go and pay him homage." When they had heard the king, they set out; and there, ahead of them, went the star that they had seen at its rising, until it stopped over the place where the child was. (2:1-9)

The magi's search for the star ended at Joseph's home. Despite the story depicted in holiday school plays and children's books, in Matthew's gospel, Mary and Joseph did not wander, looking for a place to have their child, nor did they take refuge in a stable or a manger. They were at home in Bethlehem, presumably comfortable. Powerful and symbolic gifts, represented by the magi and their gold, frankincense and myrrh, came to them—much as the dream had come to Joseph.

The gifts hold profound significance in Matthew's gospel. They were brought by the wisest of men from the East who were following heavenly and prophesied signs. As the precise and essential components of the most important rituals at The Great Temple, frankincense and myrrh were as costly as the gold used for the Temple's vessels. The oil for anointing contained the highly aromatic resin of myrrh, and frankincense only burned for the highest sacrificial offerings.

With these precious materials, Matthew symbolically transfers the components of the old physical Temple to the infant Jesus, the

Messiah and messenger of the new, inner Temple. By emphasizing the genealogy of the holy lineage—the angel who announced the birth to Joseph, and the magi, who, with their gifts anointed the baby Jesus as the Messiah—Matthew made sure that every Messianic Jew in Antioch clearly understood that Yahweh had granted His blessing and power to the new Lord. For added emphasis, Matthew incorporates another dream vision, which cautioned against a return to Herod's realm, filled with fear and out-of-date tradition.

When they saw that the star had stopped, they were overwhelmed with joy. On entering the house, they saw the child with Mary his mother; and they knelt down and paid him homage. Then, opening their treasure chests, they offered him gifts of gold, frankincense, and myrrh. (2:10-11)

...And having been warned in a dream not to return to Herod, they left for their own country by another road. (2:12)

How does the story of the magi at Jesus' birth fold itself into our lives? First, we have the image of the star as a metaphor for a spirit that guides us. It has, after all, endured through all these ages, firmly embedded in our language, and our psyches. The word disaster literally means dis-star, to be separated from one's star, from one's inner guidance. We need to recover this understanding now. We face *disaster* when we are separated from our deep wisdom.

And disaster is not too strong a word—new inspiration is rarely welcome at first. Dangers abound. Herod was relentless in his determined efforts to locate the threat represented by Jesus. He wanted to protect the center of his power. Similarly, our fears and ignorance will threaten the nascent life within us. Fear moves in hidden places and holds secrets. It is quiet, sneaky and relentless.

The fears we feel at our personal new birth mirror the difficulties of Jesus' arrival. Ours is equally unexpected, and also a home birth.

The spiritual journey begins in the middle of our usual, ordinary life. We have no exotic locales to distract us. We are usually alone, or feel so. What we have thought to be our normal world has crumbled, turned completely upside down and become chaos. Still, we have somehow heard our invitation to a new life, mustered our courage, and despite our trepidation, marched on.

But our difficulties have continued unabated. The messengers of the King of Fear, our Ego, are still on the hunt and dog our every step. In the midst of our disorientation, however, the magi will visit us, as they did the child Jesus. We don't know what form they will take, nor what specific gifts of wisdom they will bring. They may be small—a piece of the past resolved—or very large—an unshakeable communication with Inner Spirit—but they are always precious and powerful. And they are unique tools for our journey that will hold the same prominence and solemnity of the ancient gold, frankincense and myrrh. If we recognize and welcome our magi, trust, courage and inspiration will arrive as well. Recognize them, learn them, practice with them. As we gain proficiency in their use, their power will grow in us; they will become steadily more useful, fully integrated, components of our transformation.

Returning to Pain: The Flight to Egypt and Galilee

After Jesus' birth, an angel came again to Joseph, telling him to take Mary and the tiny, defenseless new baby away from the comfort of their home. Even more distressing, the angel instructed Joseph that he should take them to Egypt, the place of Jewish slavery, a place of deep danger, of historical alienation and pain. Surely, Joseph felt that he had again received an enormous, incomprehensible— even mistaken—charge.

Although Joseph acceded to these instructions, his trials were not over. Herod died, and Joseph might have safely returned home to Bethlehem, but once more an angel came in a dream and told him he was still to remain, separated from his parents and siblings. Matthew's audience would have understood the extreme nature of this command that flew in the face of all custom and the deepest of responsibilities felt by a man of his time. To leave one's family was tantamount to abandonment, a sure sign that one's ancestors had been cursed and one's descendants would be shamed. For the third time, Joseph bore the burden of a horrible requirement he could not possibly understand.

Yet once again, Joseph obeyed the angel, and leaving Egypt, chose Nazareth, in Galilee, as his new destination. Nazareth was a distant northern region considered by southerners like Joseph to be a crude, heathen, poverty-stricken, undesirable place. The Messiahians would have empathized with Joseph, since they too had made decisions that led them to a place far away from familiar and cherished traditions, which had thrown their inner lives into similar turmoil.

Now after they had left, an angel of the Lord appeared to Joseph in a dream and said, "Get up, take the child and his mother, and flee to Egypt, and remain there until I tell you; for Herod is about to search for the child, to destroy him." Then Joseph got up, took the child and his mother by night, and went to Egypt, and remained there until the death of Herod. This was to fulfill what had been spoken by the Lord through the prophet, "Out of Egypt I have called my son." When Herod saw that he had been tricked by the wise men, he was infuriated, and he sent and killed all the children in and around Bethlehem who were two years old or under, according to the time that he had learned from the wise men. Then was fulfilled what had been spoken through the prophet Jeremiah: "A voice was heard in Ramah, wailing and loud lamentation, Rachel weeping for her children; she refused to be consoled, because they are no more." When Herod died, an angel of the Lord suddenly appeared in a dream to Joseph in Egypt and said, "Get up, take the child and his mother, and go to the land of Israel, for those who were seeking the child's life are dead." Then Joseph got up, took the child and his mother, and went to the land of Israel. But when he heard that Archelaus was ruling over Judea in place of his father Herod, he was afraid to go there. And after being warned in a dream, he went away to the district of Galilee. There he made his home in a town called Nazareth, so that what had been spoken through the prophets might be fulfilled, "He will be called a Nazorean." (2:13-23)

———— ∞ ————

The angel's instruction to Joseph that he return to Egypt is one of the most profound and beautiful of Matthew's passages, perhaps because we can relate so deeply to the truths it holds. Our angel, our inner voice, will also come to us in stillness. It will tell us we must hurry back into our Egypt, our place of inner wounding. It will tell us that we must psychologically take our whole selves—our inner child *and* our parent—when we make that most difficult trek. In this exile, we will discover and examine our early pain, and then root it out, no matter how difficult that is or how long it takes.

And it might take awhile. The strength of our resolve may well turn out to be measured like Joseph's, in patience and fidelity, by our willingness to endure and remain vigilant as time passes and old understandings die. Only through our commitment to this process can we safe-keep the precious nativity we hold. This is the first and critical part of the agreement we made with ourselves when we accepted quadratos. We took on the responsibility to make the journey, but also to be its guardians.

Will we yield to our inner voice and accept the necessary exile? Will we risk living in a foreign and very uncomfortable place? Will we honor the promises we made to ourselves? The magi and Joseph all went into the unknown, following a star, listening to an angel. Our course up the veiled mountain likewise feels unknown, mysterious, frightening, but it is the gestation of the Messiah's birth in us, and I tell you that our feet fall securely on a well-worn path.

Walk onward. Trust!

Repentance and Blessing: Jesus' Baptism

Next in this gospel is the appearance of John the Baptist, who is in "the wilderness of Judea." Antiochians knew this wilderness lay below and south of the old Temple mount in Jerusalem, in the direction of Egypt. They remembered the fate of the Temple, the murder of the priests, the ensuing despair encountered by the Jewish people and that the great city had fallen into wildness. Yet John the Baptist called out that the kingdom of heaven—the reign of Spirit—was near. And he called for repentance!

These words must have puzzled the Jews in Antioch. They may well have asked, "What could he possibly mean? Wasn't the destruction of our Temple enough? How deep must our suffering be, and how can our despair bring the Messiah nearer? Could these words mean that we ourselves have to repent? Why? Surely the disasters that have befallen us were not of our making!" This confusion was precisely Matthew's intention.

In Matthew's gospel, John used the word "repent." The choice is significant. The root of "repentance" is the Greek word *poina*, which means pain. Historically, this word took three linguistic forks. One was *poine*, referring to legal compensation, and later, to expiation and punishment. Another was *poena*, meaning the taking of vengeance. The third, *poenire*, took the meaning of conscience and absolution, becoming the word "repentance" (and also became part of "penitentiary," which meant "house of correction").

Matthew's choice of words conveys an understanding that repentance is a correction of one's conscience—an act of personal, voluntary, inner transformation—very different from the frequently held view that repentance connotes punishment, or vengeance. I believe Matthew intended the Jews of Antioch to understand that they had to repent in order to mark the change from their old ways to new ways that would generate greater meaning and vitality in their lives.

In those days John the Baptist appeared in the wilderness of Judea, proclaiming, "Repent, for the kingdom of heaven has come near. This is the one of whom the prophet Isaiah spoke when he said, 'The voice of one crying out in the wilderness: Prepare the way of the Lord, make his paths straight.'" (3:1-3)

John's ensuing ritual of repentance, the baptisms, took place at the Jordan River, just east of the city of Jericho, precisely where the Hebrews had crossed into the Promised Land. It is important to understand that the actual ritual of washing in this gospel is not the same practiced today by Christians. The ritual Matthew refers to is first century Judaic "baptism," an ancient ritual that represented a moral cleansing and was directly connected to the core history of the Jewish people, which today, Jews refer to as *mikvah.*

In Matthew's telling, John the Baptist stood at the very same place at the Jordan, and asked for a reverse journey. Gathered at the river were multitudes from Jerusalem and Judea, places of power and privilege. Among them were Sadducees and Pharisees, even more elevated levels of society. Matthew takes careful and precise aim. These two groups in Antioch supported the "old order." The remnant Sadducees advocated a return to Temple worship while the Pharisees, who had become the leaders of Judaism outside Jerusalem, sought to centralize Judaism under a codified law and strict ritual observance.

John cried out, "Repent!" as a call for a commitment to profound change, a deep journey of correction. He invited the gathered multitudes to enter the river and again accept a time of exile from their historic communities, for the sake of their beliefs. Going further, he challenged the elite groups, harshly calling them a "brood of vipers," speaking of "wrath" and fire and burning. He even denied their claim to the lineage of Abraham. In this way, Matthew warns the Jews of Antioch that if they hold to the old Temple and its traditions, they choose a sure path to destruction—one that would equal the quick and painful death of a viper's bite. No past glories would protect them. All would perish. All would burn.

At the same time, Matthew uses John's voice to send a dramatic message of hope: "The new Temple has arrived. Abraham's true lineage is through Joseph to Jesus. Leave. Face completely away from the comfort of the old, accept your insecurities and walk forward. Enter the water and repent. Be corrected. You will be cleansed of your desires to hold on to your yesterdays. Repent and allow Spirit's heart within you to beat anew!"

Now John wore clothing of camel's hair with a leather belt around his waist, and his food was locusts and wild honey. Then the people of Jerusalem and all Judea were going out to him, and all the region along the Jordan, and they were baptized by him in the river Jordan, confessing their sins. But when he saw many Pharisees and Sadducees coming for baptism, he said to them, "You brood of vipers! Who warned you to flee from the wrath to come? Bear fruit worthy of repentance. Do not presume to say to yourselves, 'We have Abraham as our ancestor'; for I tell you, God is able from these stones to raise up children to Abraham. Even now the ax is lying at the root of the trees; every tree therefore that does not bear good fruit is cut down and thrown into the fire." (3:4-10)

Matthew recounts that Jesus arrived "from Galilee" in the north, where Joseph and Mary lived in exile, to join John's baptism gathering at the Jordan. John felt himself unworthy to baptize his Messiah, seeing him as an exalted presence and he resisted performing the ritual. Jesus, however, insisted that John serve, making the point that correction was a necessity for all, even the Christ—and that indeed, he had come as the exemplar of an inner truth, of "all righteousness." John consented, and Jesus entered the water. Coming up out of the water Jesus beheld a great vision. The heavens opened and the Spirit of God arrived "like the dove." Again, Matthew carefully chooses a highly resonant metaphor for the Antiochian Jews, reminding them of the dove that returned to Noah on the ark holding an olive leaf in its beak, heralding the appearance of "new land" after the flood.

Matthew uses the language of Genesis, replacing fear-filled visions with images of hope and love. Genesis described heaven as a dome, separated into the waters above and the waters below. If the dome opened, waters would certainly flood down and the earth would certainly be destroyed, as it was for Noah. In this new vision, designed for wavering Hebrew hearts, and particularly for those who believed the end of the world was imminent, Matthew offers a different ending: "If you repent, you will receive the blessing of a loving God. You will be called Beloved."

Then Jesus came from Galilee to John at the Jordan, to be baptized by him. John would have prevented him, saying, "I need to be baptized by you, and do you come to me?" But Jesus answered him, "Let it be so now; for it is proper for us in this way to fulfill all righteousness." Then he consented. And when Jesus had been baptized, just as he came up from the water, suddenly the heavens were opened to him and he saw the Spirit of God descending like a dove and alighting on him. And a voice from heaven said, "This is my Son, the Beloved, with whom I am well pleased." (3:13-17)

What does John's call to "Repent!" mean to us on the first path of quadratos? It reminds us that we each have inner voices of Sadducees and Pharisees that chatter within each of us like a nest of "brooding vipers." They roil and breed ceaselessly. They are our woundedness and fear of change. In their grip, we know only one answer, and are unable to entertain a new question. The poison held in their terrible fangs will kill any possibility of the new life we are trying to discover— quickly, silently and certainly. We must make the vital decision to become aware of these outworn inner voices and recognize that they no longer serve us. Then we must respectfully dismiss them. We must "repent" and walk in a new direction.

When Jesus, the Messiah, insisted that John perform the baptism, we are reminded that Jesus the Christ is an exemplar of our own individual journey. Inner correction is an individual responsibility to be welcomed, and if the opportunity arises where there is help, and community participation, so much the better. In the first path of quadratos, our need to confront the dilemmas of the past gives this personal responsibility particular prominence. This responsibility never ceases, of course, but one of the greatest blessings of quadratos is that as it circles back through our lives again and again, our ability to detect the need for correction increases. As this happens, thankfully, so does our capacity and comfort level in completing the task.

As Matthew has, we should call particular attention to the role of taking concrete—even public—action to mark our decision. Many established religious rituals began with this purpose, but we can certainly craft our own. Even if they remain private, or are shared only with a single friend, these acts reinforce our intention and provide an external marker which we can refer to in times of trial. If we choose a more public acknowledgment, we benefit even more, because our chosen community will stand beside us and be marshaled in our support.

The most important communication Matthew sends to us across the centuries comes at the very end of Jesus' vision. It is the gorgeous word spoken by the voice from heaven to Jesus, who stands in our stead. "Beloved," the voice pronounced. "Beloved, with whom I am well pleased." What a remarkable message to hear in our first path, when we are not always feeling very pleased, or particularly lovable. We need this message, and we need to hold it tightly, and to remember it. This is the firm foundation of quadratos, and of our journey: we are not alone, and we are loved. These are the words that can sustain us as we continue to make our way up the treacherous and rocky path.

Saying No to Illusion: The Temptations

The gospel next recounts that immediately after receiving his vision and hearing God's blessing, Jesus was led into the wilderness.

Again, Matthew is speaking to the internal experience of the Messianic Jews who had voluntarily entered a spiritual wilderness. Their choice to follow Jesus as the Messiah had led to the sacrifice of friends, family, community and tradition and, naturally, they had to contend with a strong sense of isolation and abandonment.

And a voice from heaven said, "This is my Son, the Beloved, with whom I am well pleased." Then Jesus was led up by the Spirit into the wilderness to be tempted by the devil. (3:17-4:1)

After fasting for forty days in the wilderness, Jesus became famished and in his deep exhaustion, "the tempter" arrived. When the tempter came to Jesus, he immediately challenged him to make bread from stones to assuage his hunger. Jesus ignored the challenge, completely rejecting the tempter. He refused to participate in a meaningless demonstration of power and maintained that better nourishment would be found through Spirit, in "every word that comes from the mouth of God." Matthew is telling the Messiahians, equally wearied after the fall of the Temple, that they are at risk of a similar temptation. In the first century, bread was everyone's daily staple, and Matthew intends the stones to represent the building blocks of the old Temple, which lay scattered.

He fasted forty days and forty nights, and afterwards he was famished. The tempter came and said to him, "If you are the Son of God, command these stones to become loaves of bread." But he answered, "It is written, 'One does not live by bread alone, but by every word that comes from the mouth of God.'" (4:2-4)

The tempter came a second time and placed Jesus atop "the temple." This time, he asked Jesus to prove his divinity by throwing himself from the great height without harm. In effect, the tempter whispered to Jesus, "Surely your God is not a God of such pain. Surely the 'Beloved' would not have to suffer so." Matthew speaks directly to the newly converted Messiahians in this passage, knowing that they were particularly vulnerable to this temptation. They must have found it very difficult to reconcile the pain they were experiencing with their understanding of being "loved by God."

Then the devil took him to the holy city and placed him on the pinnacle of the temple, saying to him, "If you are the Son of God, throw yourself down; for it is written 'He will command his angels concerning you,' and 'On their hands they will bear you up, so that you will not dash your foot against a stone.'" Jesus said to him, "Again it is written, 'Do not put the Lord your God to the test.'"(4:5-7)

In the third trial, Matthew offers another clear-eyed vision of the temptations the Messiahians faced. Again, he evokes the fallen Temple. The devil placed Jesus on a very high mount and showed him "the kingdoms of the world and their splendor." He offered Jesus the glittering temptation to set himself above others, as a "special" or specially anointed man.

This temptation of self-righteousness—a risk to which all "new believers" are especially susceptible—would also have resonated with the Messianic Jews in their time of external chaos and internal trial. In this allegory, "the devil," preying on the anxiety of fear and separation, promises Jesus great treasures if only he'll take a few small steps toward worshiping him.

Again, the devil took him to a very high mountain and showed him all the kingdoms of the world and their splendor; and he said to him, "All these I will give you, if you will fall down and worship me." Jesus said to him, "Away with you, Satan! for it is written, 'Worship the Lord your God, and serve only him.'" Then the devil left him, and suddenly angels came and waited on him. (4:8-11)

Matthew's temptations were not just on target for Antioch—they are the perfect stories for us on the first path of quadratos. Emotionally, we find ourselves in a strange and unaccustomed place—a mountain path, a wilderness. Most of us have been taught by our families and culture that this inner wilderness is some kind of rigorous test we must pass to become worthy enough to earn the deep voice of love. Matthew reverses this belief. Hearing the "voice of love" is only a matter of opening our hearts to an ever-present invitation. God's call challenges us to walk through this bleak landscape so that we may get to a place where that love will mature. We will be tested, certainly, but our tests will arise as we attempt to remove the obstacles to love within ourselves. Indeed, from this perspective, each crisis we meet is an invitation. As we succeed, in small steps, the elation we discover along the way will help to sustain our resolve.

As we make our way through these challenges, we too will become famished, exhausted and susceptible to temptation, just as Jesus did. It is when we are most exhausted, when we feel we have reached the limits of what we can do, or endure, that Jesus' three temptations will become most clear to us.

The illusion proffered by the first temptation might be called, "Why deny myself this pleasure?" It calls out: "Why not convert 'useless stones' into feeling better? Why not take that drink? Why not escape my intention by burying myself in family responsibilities, or work?" We need to recognize the real fears and insecurities that reside within these questions and the pitfalls that acting on them represent.

The second temptation whines. Its imploring voice says, "Surely this path is not about suffering?" When we listen to this voice, we will try to maintain our lives in a rosy world where we never truly face pain, only deny it. We indulge in fantasies, longing for worlds without unfairness or conflict. Sometimes, we slip into the role of victim, identifying all of our pain as coming from outside ourselves, from "them." Our confused ego-mind offers us this illusion as it struggles to stay in control.

If we allow this cycle to continue, then the tragic, inevitable next step is a whisper that suggests to us that, "If this is from God, then God has abandoned us, and we should abandon God." All of us who have suffered tragedy or trauma or loss will recognize the power of this suggestion and the risk of accepting it, but if we are to move toward our inner freedom, we must resist.

The third temptation may be the most pernicious, because it can be very, very sneaky. It tells our ego-mind that it can be in charge, that it can be "special," elevated above others, a "king." It tries to subvert our elation and convert our sense of being "Beloved" into being "most Beloved." Its vehicle is self-righteousness. When we begin to believe that our personal and hard-won certainties are the only truth for anyone other than ourselves, we diminish the experience and inner wisdom of others. We have begun to "worship" the devil of division. We are on a grim course that leads inevitably into a type of grandiosity that seeks to elevate ourselves at the expense of others—and avoid pain through a false sense of merit or privilege.

This third temptation affects our world on a daily basis. It can start with something as simple as the desire of a child for a particular kind of clothes, or toy, so he or she will feel more "special," be more popular and hence "better" than his or her peers. As these children grow into adulthood, many of them can readily become convinced that outer signs and material goods equate to entitlement. Communities divide instead of unite as walls go up around "gated developments." Mental and emotional gates follow the physical gates. And on both sides of the walls, people speak of "them."

In religion, we see the same pattern. One church or synagogue or mosque—equally self-elevated and separated from full human brotherhood—condemns the practices of another, predicting God's wrath and shunning, even killing, the members of another sect it perceives to be offending. In global politics, one country calls another "evil" and acts on that perception; yet in its self-righteousness, it employs policies as extreme as those of the opponent it condemns. It even makes war. All of this is the "temptation" that Jesus resisted, and Matthew's inspired prose condemns.

This is not ivory-tower idealism of any kind. There are real differences between people. There are genuine and valuable distinctions, true merit and earned rewards. There are a multitude of problems created by these differences that must be addressed pragmatically. However, there is also a simultaneous truth: when our inner selves convert distinctions into a perceived right to diminish others, we are not on a holy path. We are, as the third temptation tries so hard to lure us to do, serving the devil. God, the real Mystery we seek, does not devalue our differences. God holds us all as equally Beloved.

Another caution: when we find ourselves praying a prayer of restoration, asking for a return of the past, or our old, comfortable ways, even if it is a very small request, we should immediately stop and reflect upon our motives. Most often, these prayers are really an attempt to quell our uncertainty. While this is certainly understandable on the first path, and we can view it self-compassionately, we must realize that we cannot go back. Our uncertainty is necessary and holy. If we dispel it, we cannot avoid destroying Mystery also—the very thing we seek. Mystery cannot be cut down to human size. It cannot be made comprehensible and monolithic. It is Mystery. It is God.

A genuine path opens before us, not in the direction of greater control, but toward greater intimacy. It releases us into learning to live within great unknowing, rather than attempting to exert power over it. The unknowing forms our journey, and the greatest perils of our pilgrimage are the ways we choose to contend with fear. Matthew's allegories of Jesus and the tempter awaken us to the greatest of these risks.

Climbing with a Practical Heart: The Sermon on the Mount

Chapters five through twenty-five of Matthew's gospel comprise the heart of what have come to be called Jesus' Wisdom Teachings. The opening portion of this enormous section, chapters five, six and seven, is known as the "Sermon on the Mount," and contains the Lord's Prayer. Its core teachings, "The Beatitudes," are found in chapter five. We will study these closely.

Chapters eight through twenty-five are largely composed of lessons called the Parables, which amplify and elucidate the previous instruction. Matthew included them as additional tools for those in Antioch, and designed them as conundrums, an ancient method of wisdom teaching. Each is intentionally structured to confound, to tie the rational mind into knots, thereby assisting in the deconstruction of old ways of thinking. The theory holds that while the mind is thus occupied, something may be loosened in the heart, thereby allowing for the grace of fuller understanding. They are lengthy, and we will not study them here, but I strongly recommend you read them. They can be valuable in wrestling with the new ways that begin to arise in the first path—and they contain beautiful poetic passages.

In chapter five, we see that Matthew, ever cognizant of the symbolic efficacy of the Great Temple, sets Jesus' great sermon atop a high mount in Galilee. Seated, in the expected posture of an elder teaching in the Temple, the Messiah began speaking. This mountain had no name. It was not one of the traditional Jewish holy places, and he was not in any structure—not in a physical temple of any kind. The words of wisdom did not remonstrate or demand in the traditional manner, but instead they tumbled out poetically, lovingly, reflecting a new way of teaching.

The section begins with the lyrical verses of the Beatitudes. Their poetic words transmit a nine-fold blessing from Jesus to his disciples and to the later adherents whom Matthew addresses. Each of the nine couplets invokes supportive and constructive attitudes of heart—practical assistance for beginning and withstanding the inner challenges of a spiritual journey.

When Jesus saw the crowds, he went up the mountain; and after he sat down, his disciples came to him. Then he began to speak, and taught them, saying:

"Blessed are the poor in spirit, for theirs is the kingdom of heaven.

Blessed are those who mourn, for they will be comforted.

Blessed are the meek, for they will inherit the earth.

Blessed are those who hunger and thirst for righteousness, for they will be filled.

Blessed are the merciful, for they will receive mercy.

Blessed are the pure in heart, for they will see God.

Blessed are the peacemakers, for they will be called children of God.

Blessed are those who are persecuted for righteousness' sake, for theirs is the kingdom of heaven.

Blessed are you when people revile you and persecute you and utter all kinds of evil against you falsely on my account.

Rejoice and be glad, for your reward is great in heaven, for in the same way they persecuted the prophets who were before you." (5:1-12)

After reciting the Beatitudes, Jesus continued with a clear and uncompromising teaching, found in none of the other gospels. In it, he set down new ways of evaluating and dealing with traditional practices. In this section, like a repeated chant, Jesus recited: "You have heard it said to those of ancient times..." and then he would insert a particular religious or cultural practice. Then Jesus would say, "But I say to you..." and provide his new, expanded interpretation of that practice. Matthew uses these revolutionary words of Jesus to directly address the Messianic Jews of Antioch, who found themselves deeply embattled by the Pharisees and Sadducees.

Matthew has a twofold intention. First, he wants to make it apparent that perfect religious practice would not bring the Messiah, no matter what those in Antioch "have heard said." The Messiah had already arrived, so anyone who was still calling for perfection was clearly wrong. Antiochians could relinquish any onerous burden of perfection (and any sense of shame that it generated) with a clear conscience.

His second goal is to convince the Messiahians of the need for new ways of thinking about rules of conduct. Just because a respected external authority establishes a code of behavior does not make it correct. Meaningless acquiescence is not a holy course, because a genuinely holy path requires individual responsibility, effort and scrutiny. As Jesus the Messiah taught, learning, reflection and evaluation reveal the true essence of the "rules," enabling them to become a meaningful practice flowing naturally from love and compassion.

"Do not think that I have come to abolish the law or the prophets; I have come not to abolish but to fulfill... (5:17)

"You have heard that it was said to those of ancient times, 'You shall not murder; and whoever murders shall be liable to judgment.' But I say to you that if you are angry with a brother or sister, you will be liable to judgment; and if you insult a brother or sister, you will be liable to the council; and if you say, 'You fool,' you will be liable to the hell of fire..." (5:21-22)

"You have heard that it was said, 'You shall not commit adultery.' But I say to you that everyone who looks at a woman with lust has already committed adultery with her in his heart..." (5:27-28)

"Again, you have heard that it was said to those of ancient times, 'You shall not swear falsely, but carry out the vows you have made to the Lord.' But I say to you, Do not swear at all, either by heaven, for it is the throne of God, or by the earth, for it is his footstool." (5:33-35)

"You have heard that it was said, 'An eye for an eye and a tooth for a tooth.' But I say to you, Do not resist an evildoer. But if anyone strikes you on the right cheek, turn the other also; and if anyone wants to sue you and take your coat, give your cloak as well; and if anyone forces you to go one mile, go also the second mile. Give to everyone who begs from you, and do not refuse anyone who wants to borrow from you." (5:38-42)

"You have heard that it was said, 'You shall love your neighbor and hate your enemy.' But I say to you, Love your enemies and pray for those who persecute you, so that you may be children of your Father in heaven; for he makes his sun rise on the evil and on the good, and sends rain on the righteous and on the unrighteous..." (5:43-45)

The wisdom teachings in Matthew contain such an abundance of sensible counsel that we would do well to keep them close. They are a poetic guide to the promises and the dangers that greet us on the first path. The recommendations and responses they hold are truly Be-Attitudes that challenge us to:

- Accept that we do not and will not know results in advance. We will often feel "poor in spirit."
- Make farewells to our yesterdays. Embrace the grief we feel.
- Be meek. Yielding to exile will yield the riches of Spirit.

- Know that our true hunger and thirst are for Spirit, and only Spirit, despite all trials and temptations.
- Greet all we encounter, within and without, in mercy. Mercy derives from *merces,* a Latin word that translates as "reward." (It continued into French as *merci,* meaning thanks, or gratitude.) Reap the rewards of gratitude.
- Be full of heart. Do not seek to remove any thought, any feeling or any person from our inner life. Each is an aspect of Spirit. Welcome them.
- Believe in "Jeru-Shalom" as a place of peace that can be heard arising in the midst of differing voices.
- Accept inner and outer hardship for the sake of living a new life in the presence of God. Power and applause is not what we seek. Our journey will lead instead to humility and service.
- Do not expect esteem. Meet conflict—and meet it with respect and love.

The nine Beatitudes reflect the diverse parts of a harmonious whole. They bend around and touch each other. As the very heart of Jesus' teachings, their practice opens us to compassion. If we are able to place these on our hearts, walk with them on our feet, hold them in our hands, and seal them in our thoughts, we will have more insight along our journey. They will become our walking staff and guide for the arduous times we will face.

We can certainly find equal relevance in the rest of the Sermon on the Mount. Each one of us has "heard it said"—by parents, by friends, by society, by religious institutions—that we ought to "do this" or "avoid that." Unreflectively, we may have accepted or rejected these rules. Jesus' words ask us to become more conscious. He tells us that truth is not found on the surface. We are encouraged to explore both the original purpose and meanings of the things we have been told, as well as their genuine truth and relevance in our hearts and lives today.

We have talked about the risk of returning to older, seemingly simpler, ways, but an equal peril lurks within this first path of quadratos: the urge to rush to the opposite position. Our ego-mind can just as readily deceive us into thinking that all of yesterday's wisdom is empty folly—that nothing we have ever learned or been told has merit or benefit; that we are without guidance. In this place, isolation and despair can loom large. Remember, though, that this is only a trick, not a truth. Quadratos requires that we ignore these deceptions and dig deeper, explore further. Although many people and institutions have become protectors of empty practices, there are others who still hold truthful, living attitudes of heart. We must discover these and endeavor to claim them in our own personal way. In this challenge, the tools of discernment that we will learn from the full process of quadratos will become our most steadfast ally.

Meeting Betrayal with Friendship: The Passion

Each of the four gospels has an account of Jesus' final days and death. These accounts are commonly called "The Passion," deriving from the Latin root *pati-*, which means "to suffer, or endure." Each gospel recounts the Passion story in a different way—no less dramatic, no less inspirational, no less spiritually valuable—but very, very different. In each telling, the community to whom the story is directed is able to understand Jesus the Christ's death and resurrection as the necessary and logical culmination of the lessons preceding it in the gospel. Furthermore, the circumstances of the Passion itself are set by each writer in a way that enables that community to most poignantly and personally internalize Jesus' experience and make its connections to their own.

In Matthew's gospel, remember that the Jewish community of Antioch was grieving, argumentative and anxious. Matthew's passion account is directed specifically at the small, beleaguered group of Messianic Jews and is designed to provide very specific guidance. Throughout this recitation, Jesus the Christ is the exemplar of remaining emotionally and spiritually present in a time of bitter trial, loss and uncertainty.

Arriving in Jerusalem

After preaching the Sermon on the Mount, Jesus continued to teach in Galilee and Judea, telling stories and challenging the authority of the Temple at every turn. The chief priests and Temple elders in Jerusalem were quite naturally becoming increasingly incensed over the potential rebellion these teachings represented. They felt the power, authority and perquisites of the Temple were at risk. Jesus finally arrived in Jerusalem itself, and the Temple leaders decided it was time to dispose of the threat of this upstart teacher. But they were apprehensive. Jesus' popularity was such that they feared Rome would hold the Temple responsible should riots break out if they were to arrest him.

Overtaken by both urgency and opportunity, the authorities opted for a plan offered by Jesus' disciple, Judas. It was the time of the Feast of Unleavened Bread, the celebration today known as Passover. The plan called for the arrest of Jesus late on the first night of the festival when, distracted by the late hour and festivities, the public would hopefully have little, if any, reaction.

When Jesus had finished saying all these things, he said to his disciples, "You know that after two days the Passover is coming, and the Son of Man will be handed over to be crucified." Then the chief priests and the elders of the people gathered in the palace of the high priest, who was called Caiaphas, and they conspired to arrest Jesus by stealth and kill him. But they said, "Not during the festival, or there may be a riot among the people." (26:1-5)

In a pointed digression, Matthew takes the next few verses to tell an allegorical tale of a meal in the home of Simon the leper. During the meal, an unnamed woman arrived and anointed Jesus' head with expensive oil. A mere five verses later, he tells of the equal amount of silver Judas Iscariot received for betraying Jesus. This juxtaposition not only heightens the drama of the passion, but sends a powerful message to the Messiahians: "In times of difficulty, grief, even death, there will be opportunities—tests—that will arise. They may hold honor, or betrayal. When they come, who are you? Will you pay the cost to honor the beliefs of your soul? Or will you collect the price of shame and betray them? The expense of either will be high, and you will have to decide."

Now while Jesus was at Bethany in the house of Simon the leper, a woman came to him with an alabaster jar of very costly ointment, and she poured it on his head as he sat at the table. (26:6-7)

Then one of the twelve, who was called Judas Iscariot, went to the chief priests and said, "What will you give me if I betray him to you?" They paid him thirty pieces of silver. And from that moment he began to look for an opportunity to betray him. (26:14-16)

The Last Supper

The first verses show that Jesus was aware of his arrest and sub-sequent fate and accepted both in a matter-of-fact way that stands in startling contrast to the horrifying events that followed. The focus is on the Passover meal itself, and the conversation that ensued.

In the custom of the time, meals were served in a single, common bowl. Tearing a piece of bread to use as a scoop, each person reached into the bowl, got food, and then ate. Jesus announced that his betrayal would come from "the one who has dipped his hand into the bowl with me." These words literally specified that *everyone* at the table that night would betray him, and he did not differentiate between Judas and the other disciples.

Jesus knew *none* of the disciples were sufficiently ready, suffi-ciently mature in their faith, to be capable of constancy. He knew they would cling to their old behaviors, the old order. He knew that betrayals of all kinds would occur over and over and over again—that this was an inevitable and to-be-expected part of the early stages of the spiritual journey—and he wanted to prepare his followers for this reality. He wanted to bring them forward to the much more important lesson of "what remains to be done after betrayal?"

Everyone at the table, even Judas, responded: "Surely, not I?" Matthew notes, however, one small—but extremely significant—difference concerning Judas. Eleven disciples addressed Jesus as "Lord," in recognition of Jesus' higher nature and authority, but Judas addressed Jesus as "Rabbi." In that time, rabbis were not the specially educated heads of congregations that they are now. They were largely self-appointed teachers who had the capacity to attract a following, and were often completely unlettered. With this address, Judas therefore minimized Jesus' station, treating him as simply another man. Judas could, with impunity, ignore and even disrespect, a mere rabbi. It is likely that this is more a message to the Messiahians than an accurate historical detail. Matthew is probably much more concerned that those in Antioch acknowledge Jesus the Christ as "Lord" instead of "Rabbi" than Jesus would have been. Nonetheless, it is an important distinction in this gospel with respect to the character of Judas.

On the first day of Unleavened Bread the disciples came to Jesus, saying, "Where do you want us to make the preparations for you to eat the Passover?" He said, "Go into the city to a certain man, and say to him, 'The Teacher says, My time is near; I will keep the Passover at your house with my disciples.'" So the disciples did as Jesus had directed them, and they prepared the Passover meal. (26:17-19)

When it was evening, he took his place with the twelve; and while they were eating, he said, "Truly I tell you, one of you will betray me." And they became greatly distressed and began to say to him one after another, "Surely not I, Lord?" He answered, "The one who has dipped his hand into the bowl with me will betray me. The Son of Man goes as it is written of him, but woe to that one by whom the Son of Man is betrayed! It would have been better for that one not to have been born." Judas, who betrayed him, said, "Surely not I, Rabbi?" He replied, "You have said so." (26:20-25)

After the meal, Jesus went with the remaining disciples to the Mount of Olives, knowing he would be arrested there. Peter and the disciples—except Judas who had already left—once again promised their total fidelity to Jesus, even in death. Yet within a few hours, they were all to desert him. The irony of this repeated promise added further to the litany of betrayals in Matthew's story.

When they had sung the hymn, they went out to the Mount of Olives. Then Jesus said to them, "You will all become deserters because of me this night; for it is written, 'I will strike the shepherd, and the sheep of the flock will be scattered.' But after I am raised up, I will go ahead of you to Galilee." Peter said to him, "Though all become deserters because of you, I will never desert you." Jesus said to him, "Truly I tell you, this very night, before the cock crows, you will deny me three times." Peter said to him, "Even though I must die with you, I will not deny you." And so said all the disciples. (26:30-35)

The Garden of Gethsemane sat atop the Mount of Olives. The word *gethsemane* means a place where olives are pressed, and using it here as the named location clearly reiterates the core message of this gospel—the effort, strain and attentiveness necessary to produce new oil of balm, of anointing, of blessing. After hearing their promises, Jesus selected three of his disciples to join him in the garden. He chose the most loyal and experienced of them, the same three who had previously accompanied him up another mountain and experienced a vision of Jesus "transfigured" as the Christ (17:1-13). Jesus requested they remain with him and stay awake as he prayed. Three times the Messiah prayed, "If it is possible, let this cup pass from me; yet not what I want but what you want." Three times the disciples, tired and distressed, proved unable to stay awake and fell soundly into sleep. Jesus remonstrated with Peter that he was not yet strong enough to endure real tests of faith.

An often-debated question arises here about which cup Jesus prayed not to drink. Earlier, at the Passover meal, Jesus had said he would not take wine again "until that day when I will drink it new with you in my Father's kingdom" (26:29). Yet in this verse, perhaps only an hour later, Jesus prayed to let "this cup" go by if possible. Did he mean the cup of his imminent death, or a metaphorical cup of bitterness caused by the desertion of his intimate friends and disciples? We cannot know for certain. However, because Matthew consistently emphasizes betrayal and its consequences throughout the passion (as well as Jesus' almost nonchalant acceptance of his fate), I believe that the prayer was metaphorical, that it asked for release from inner pain over abandonment and was not a prayer to avoid his death.

Then Jesus went with them to a place called Gethsemane; and he said to his disciples, "Sit here while I go over there and pray." He took with him Peter and the two sons of Zebedee, and began to be grieved and agitated. Then he said to them, "I am deeply grieved, even to death; remain here, and stay awake with me." And going a little farther, he threw himself on the ground and prayed, "My Father, if it is possible, let this cup pass from me; yet not what I want but what you want." Then he came to the disciples and found them sleeping; and he said to Peter, "So, could you not stay awake with me one hour? Stay awake and pray that you may not come into the time of trial; the spirit indeed is willing, but the flesh is weak." (26:36-41).

The Garden of Gethsemane, the Arrest and Trial

When Judas appeared at the garden with a crowd sent by the Temple authorities, he identified Jesus by kissing him, again using the word "Rabbi" and not "Lord." In return, Jesus addressed Judas as "Friend," completely embodying the principles he taught in the Sermon on the Mount. He then calmly accepted his arrest. Could there have been a more dramatic example for the divided Jewish community of Antioch of responding to betrayal and loss with equanimity and compassion?

While Jesus was still speaking, Judas, one of the twelve, arrived; with him was a large crowd with swords and clubs, from the chief priests and the elders of the people. Now the betrayer had given them a sign, saying, "The one I will kiss is the man; arrest him." At once he came up to Jesus and said, "Greetings, Rabbi!" and kissed him. Jesus said to him, "Friend, do what you are here to do." Then they came and laid hands on Jesus and arrested him. (26:47-50)

Following the arrest, the chief priests held a trial (a very different trial than we will read of in the Gospel of John). Throughout this trial, Jesus remained silent. Finally, when placed under oath, he responded to the high priest, and did not claim to be the Messiah. Consistent with Matthew's other references to prophecy, Jesus spoke instead of the "Son of Man," an implicit reference to the Hebrew Book of Daniel (7:13), which contains a vision in which Daniel saw "one who is like a human being" acting as God's agent, winning a battle for God, and restoring harmony between heaven and earth.

The chief priests were enraged when they heard Jesus predict that "the Son of Man" would sit in a place of power. His vision implied that high priests sacrificing animals on altars would become unimportant and clearly denounced the authority of the Temple. In short, Jesus foretold nothing less than a spiritual revolution.

Under oath, Jesus drew a line—and historically, he was proven correct. The presence of Jesus the Christ did, in fact, cause the inner authority of the Temple to crumble, and only a few decades later, Rome completed the job by destroying the Temple's outer shell.

Matthew, always determined to communicate this parallel to the Jews in Antioch, never missed an opportunity to reiterate: "Let your old beliefs and desire for a physical Temple go. These allegiances are outworn. They are like a heap of dry bones. Kick them aside on your path up God's mountain. Embrace the unknown. You are beloved. Do not fear."

Now the chief priests and the whole council were looking for false testimony against Jesus so that they might put him to death, but they found none, though many false witnesses came forward. At last two came forward and said, "This fellow said, 'I am able to destroy the temple of God and to build it in three days.'" The high priest stood up and said, "Have you no answer? What is it that they testify against you?" But Jesus was silent. Then the high priest said to him, "I put you under oath before the living God, tell us if you are the Messiah, the Son of God." Jesus said to him, "You have said so. But I tell you, from now on you will see the Son of Man seated at the right hand of Power and coming on the clouds of heaven." Then the high priest tore his clothes and said, "He has blasphemed! Why do we still need witnesses? You have now heard his blasphemy. What is your verdict?" They answered, "He deserves death." (26:59-66)

Betrayals continued in the Passion story. Peter, the most intimate of Jesus' disciples, fearing arrest, denied knowing Jesus on three separate occasions. However, Matthew uses his example as the opportunity for a deeper teaching. Despite his betrayal, Peter subsequently experienced not only remorse, but also self-understanding. Consequently, he remained not only a full disciple but also a witness throughout the narrative, underscoring Matthew's point to the Antiochians, that facing one's weakness with honesty and mercy leads to greater strength.

Now Peter was sitting outside in the courtyard. A servant-girl came to him and said, "You also were with Jesus the Galilean." But he denied it before all of them, saying, "I do not know what you are talking about." When he went out to the porch, another servant-girl saw him, and she said to the bystanders, "This man was with Jesus of Nazareth." Again he denied it with an oath, "I do not know the man." After a little while the bystanders came up and said to Peter, "Certainly you are also one of them, for your accent betrays you." Then he began to curse, and he swore an oath, "I do not know the man!" At that moment the cock crowed. Then Peter remembered what Jesus had said: "Before the cock crows, you will deny me three times." And he went out and wept bitterly. (26: 69-75)

Judas, meanwhile, also regretted his betrayal and returned to the priests in despair, returning to them the silver they had paid him. Without sympathy for his distress, they dismissed him contemptuously. Judas left and committed suicide. This gives Matthew a clear contrast for his audience. Peter reflected; he "remembered what Jesus had said." He acknowledged Jesus' power as greater than his own. So even though he had briefly given in to his fears, he had the stability for self-forgiveness and the capacity to move forward. He could come back to the Messiah and walk on despite his failings.

Judas, on the other hand, had successfully been tempted and lacked the inner resources to reflect beyond his own misery. He never possessed humility like Peter, but instead, stayed trapped in his arrogance. Nor did he ever develop the inner resources to reflect and "remember" in the way Peter did. When shame and despair overwhelmed him, he returned to the old ways, personified by the "chief priests and elders." Trapped in his fears, Judas never understood Jesus' invitation or his message of forgiveness, and death became the only option he could discover in the limitations of his closed imagination and heart.

Judas' suicide appears only in the Gospel of Matthew. It was a message to the Messiahians, but stands as one of the great messages in Christianity: forgiveness is always available for a believer in Jesus the Christ. The voice of love is ever-present. We are the only ones who can close the door to forgiveness, and we close it on ourselves, through our own lack of understanding.

When Judas, his betrayer, saw that Jesus was condemned, he repented and brought back the thirty pieces of silver to the chief priests and the elders. He said, "I have sinned by betraying innocent blood." But they said, "What is that to us? See to it yourself." Throwing down the pieces of silver in the temple, he departed; and he went and hanged himself. (27:3-5)

Subsequent events have a tone of increasing bitterness. The "chief priests and elders" persuaded "the crowds" to demand that the Roman governor, Pontius Pilate, grant clemency to Barabbas, another prisoner and known criminal, and sentence Jesus to death. Pilate acquiesced. Matthew frequently links "crowd" and "chief priests and elders." He used this vocabulary at Jesus' arrest, and does so again at the sentencing. This "crowd" was not just any group of people from Jerusalem, or even an innocuous group of Jews, but a specific group of Temple followers, doing the bidding of the Temple authorities—a distinction critical to our comprehension of events that follow.

After his condemnation by Pilate, Jesus was taken away and flogged. But first, the soldiers placed a scarlet robe on him. Although all four gospels record the robe, the color varies in each, reflecting the core message of that particular gospel. Matthew robes Jesus in the color of blood. Matthew wants to call attention to the implications of blood, a central component to the Jewish people and their traditional religious life. In the hour before each dawn the chief priest poured the blood of a lamb over the high altar. Jews believed that the life force of a creature or a person resided in their blood, which made it the most significant element of the animal. The meat itself was discarded and burnt.

Images of blood are woven throughout this gospel. The lengthy genealogy dramatizes the bloodline of the Messiahians. Herod shed the blood of innocents when he searched for the infant Jesus. Judas' silver, received for betraying Jesus, became known as "blood money." Pilate washed his hands of Jesus' innocent blood, and the Temple authorities and their crowd cried out: "His blood be on us and on our children!"

For centuries, this cry has been read as a curse, and used to justify the torture and killing of Jewish people. Did Matthew intend this as a curse on the Jews? All Biblical texts have many possible readings, but because of the particularly horrible uses to which this phrase has been put, I think it is very important that we analyze this thoroughly. I do not believe that Matthew intended to curse Jews or the Jewish religion at all.

My belief is based on several very obvious realities. The first is the clear metaphorical meanings Matthew has ascribed to the Temple authorities and the "crowd" of Temple followers around them. Throughout the gospel, these figures symbolize the old ways of thinking and doing. They represent groups and people who, over time, became complacent and allowed inspiration to diminish so that increasingly rigid structures could be accommodated. These same people became unreflective and obedient to authority and tradition for its own sake. So when they cry out after Pilate's decision, their words are the desperate words of a threatened belief system, which Matthew has characterized as "corrupt" and useless.

Matthew has a complete grasp of the early stages of the spiritual journey. His Passion is a profound analogy. His account tells Jesus' story, and simultaneously reveals its deeper revelation: spiritual growth requires an internal death and a renunciation of the old. In this sense, "His (Jesus') blood" would be upon the crowd (and their descendants) and when it fell upon them, it would change them. The "new blood" would transform the old. I realize that this may be an unorthodox reading of the crowd's cry. However, I find its message of encouragement and hope for the Messiahians—that their fellow Jews would eventually join them in their beliefs—to be far more consistent with Matthew's gospel than the traditional (and to me, hateful) interpretation.

The "curse" theory cannot be valid for an even greater reason: it would be completely antithetical to Jesus' consistent behavior and teachings, and certainly to Matthew's inspired gospel that recounts them. Scholars agree that the Beatitudes contain the clearest example of Jesus' principal lessons, and these explicit instructions, in my view, mandate that Matthew's messages throughout his gospel be interpreted in that spirit. Matthew wants the Messianic Jews to be transformed by love, not hampered by hate.

Now the chief priests and the elders persuaded the crowds to ask for Barabbas and to have Jesus killed. The governor again said to them, "Which of the two do you want me to release for you?" And they said, "Barabbas." Pilate said to them, "Then what should I do with Jesus who is called the Messiah?" All of them said, "Let him be crucified!" Then he asked, "Why, what evil has he done?" But they shouted all the more, "Let him be crucified!" So when Pilate saw that he could do nothing, but rather that a riot was beginning, he took some water and washed his hands before the crowd, saying, "I am innocent of this man's blood; see to it yourselves." Then the people as a whole answered, "His blood be on us and on our children!" So he released Barabbas for them; and after flogging Jesus, he handed him over to be crucified. Then the soldiers of the governor took Jesus into the governor's headquarters, and they gathered the whole cohort around him. They stripped him and put a scarlet robe on him, and after twisting some thorns into a crown, they put it on his head. They put a reed in his right hand and knelt before him and mocked him, saying, "Hail, King of the Jews!" They spat on him, and took the reed and struck him on the head. After mocking him, they stripped him of the robe and put his own clothes on him. Then they led him away to crucify him. (27:24-31)

Crucifixion and Death

Except for his preparatory prayer in Gethsemane, Matthew gives no hint that Jesus suffers, or even takes much note of the terrible events of the Passion. He responded simply and quietly to Pilate at his trial, and, it seems, responds not at all to the flogging or sustained mockery.

When the time finally came for his painful death, Jesus' demeanor still did not change. At Golgotha, the place of crucifixion, Matthew tells us that Jesus was offered gall, a bitter substance that deadens pain when mixed with wine. Jesus rejected the potion. He chose to remain fully awake, to face and feel every moment with an open mind, heart and body, unresistant to the pain. His noble behavior demonstrated the legitimacy of his place in the genealogy as "the son of David, the son of Abraham." This served as an excruciating message to Antioch: "Suffering is of value. This time is your necessary trial, your unavoidable inner death. Stay present. Stay awake to the experience. God will sustain you."

And when they came to a place called Golgotha (which means Place of a Skull), they offered him wine to drink, mixed with gall; but when he tasted it, he would not drink it. (27:33-34)

Jesus hung on the cross, where he withstood the jeers and mockery of the Temple followers. Matthew clearly references Jesus' second temptation (4:5-7), when he describes how the Temple authorities and their group at the crucifixion challenge Jesus to come down and escape his torment. Matthew makes an explicit parallel when he equates the demands of the priests, the old order, with the temptations of the devil. He unequivocally avers that the Temple is corrupt, no longer useful and obstructing the new ways. "Do you think the Pharisees abuse their power in Antioch?" Matthew asks. "Look at how the old Temple structure abused your Messiah!" No opportunity is lost to make his point.

Those who passed by derided him, shaking their heads and saying, "You who would destroy the temple and build it in three days, save yourself! If you are the Son of God, come down from the cross." In the same way the chief priests also, along with the scribes and elders, were mocking him, saying, "He saved others; he cannot save himself. He is the King of Israel; let him come down from the cross now, and we will believe in him. He trusts in God; let God deliver him now, if he wants to; for he said, 'I am God's Son.'" The bandits who were crucified with him also taunted him in the same way. (27:39-44)

As Jesus' last moments drew near, he called out the first line of Psalm 22, "My God, my God, why have you forsaken me?" To be certain it is properly identified, Matthew puts it both in its original Aramaic, as well as its translation. *(See Appendix B for the three major Aramaic/Hebrew variations of this line.)* Any devout Jew in the first century, who had prayed all his life, would have hoped to be able to pray this Psalm at his death. Its misinterpretation by some of the "crowd" (that Jesus is calling for Elijah, rather than beginning the prayer of Psalm 22) is a pejorative comment by Matthew about the crudeness of their characters and the genuineness of their piety. *(See the passion in Mark's gospel, described in Chapter 4, for more detail on Psalm 22.)*

And about three o'clock Jesus cried with a loud voice, "Eli, Eli, lema sabachthani?" that is, "My God, my God, why have you forsaken me?" When some of the bystanders heard it, they said, "This man is calling for Elijah." At once one of them ran and got a sponge, filled it with sour wine, put it on a stick, and gave it to him to drink. But the others said, "Wait, let us see whether Elijah will come to save him." Then Jesus cried again with a loud voice and breathed his last. (27:46-50)

Only the Gospel of Matthew records the next phenomenon: a great earthquake and a simultaneous tearing of "the curtain of the Temple" that occur precisely at the moment Jesus dies. The curtain shields the entrance to the Holy of Holies in the Temple, making this a powerful and climactic image for the Messianic Jews.

The Messianic Jews of Antioch could certainly relate to an earthquake, as every aspect of their lives was being shaken. Their connection to the divine must have seemed especially precarious. Without the Temple, could they still reach God, know God and see

God? Matthew's image must have awed and frightened them. Nevertheless, it also fully affirmed their hope in the blessing found at the heart of Jesus' teachings. The curtain in the Temple tore because it had lost its usefulness. The treasures, until then kept behind the curtain, now rested outside the physical Temple. The Messiah had come, and God was now omnipresent, found everywhere, within them, accessible at any time and to all believers—not just the priests. Furthermore, this cataclysmic opening had also raised the saints who would, presumably, now be available, directly, to them.

Then Jesus cried again with a loud voice and breathed his last. At that moment the curtain of the temple was torn in two, from top to bottom. The earth shook, and the rocks were split. The tombs also were opened, and many bodies of the saints who had fallen asleep were raised. (27:50-52)

Well over the threshold of the first path of quadratos and into our journey, how shall we summarize the significance of Matthew's Passion? We have been greeted with hope and grief, promise and resentment. That is the first path. We know that no matter the depth of our previous spiritual growth, each time we stand on the threshold of deep change, we will feel the sting of anxiety that marks our crossing into the new unknown. Will we choose to be awake as we hike up the mountain? Will we choose to confront our fears, even unto the death of our small beliefs and the uncompassionate corners of our most hidden hearts? Will we choose compassion—at this juncture, mostly for ourselves? And as we are able, for others?

Our first deep practice in this phase requires self-responsibility and presence. We must be "with" ourselves—mind, body and spirit—in a condition of self-honesty and openness. Although we must not descend into isolation, we cannot allow ourselves to be distracted by anything or anyone. We can take no gall. Instead, our course is prayer, and the asking for wise counsel therein.

Our second practice asks patience. We must understand that, as we walk up the mountain, we will have many missteps, many "self-betrayals." We must expect this, and meet each of these with love, instead of piling self-criticism and shame on the fragile new self that is emerging. We must call ourselves "friend." We must give ourselves permission to do what is necessary and acknowledge that even our mistakes help us on the journey of quadratos that Spirit has chosen for us. We must learn self-honor and say "thank you." When we embrace ourselves in this way, we will find the strength and freedom to go further, to use each instance as an opportunity for self-examination and discernment.

We must also aspire to choose interpretations and seek meanings in our scriptures and in our lives that promote love and openness, rather than strife and division. Jesus the Christ in Matthew curses no one. I believe it is very much past time for Christianity as a body, and Christians as individuals, to understand and accept this reality and renounce its ancient, unfounded hatreds. Indeed, any vestiges of these feelings within us represent only our own fear and resistance to a life lived in love.

⎯⎯⎯ ⚇ ⎯⎯⎯

Moving Past Tribe: The Resurrection of the Messiah

Just as there are four distinct Passion accounts in the gospels, there are four individual resurrection accounts. Each story of the resurrection serves to both resolve and carry forward into practice the core set of concerns on which the writer has focused.

Matthew's resurrection account, written to its Antiochian "beginners" in the midst of great uncertainty, is a buoyant conclusion to his gospel. Matthew has given the Messiahians the teachings of Jesus—in words that are inspiring, yet uncompromising. He has shown Jesus the Messiah tranquilly enduring the travails and abuse of his trial and crucifixion, even his death. At the end of the gospel, the Resurrection holds out the vision of a world that can become reality if the challenge of Jesus' transcendent example can be met.

After Jesus' burial, as both Mary Magdalene and Mary, "the mother of James and Joseph," waited by the tomb, Matthew tells of a second earthquake and the simultaneous rolling back of the tomb-stone by an angel. Sitting on the stone, the angel proclaimed Jesus' resurrection saying, "He has been raised from the dead, and indeed he is going ahead of you to Galilee; there you will see him." Like the earlier combination of earthquake and curtain-tearing, this reiterated Matthew's central message: "God, the promise of the Messiah, has moved out of the Temple, out of the tomb. You are invited to a new and larger life. You are invited to make a journey without end."

After the sabbath, as the first day of the week was dawning, Mary Magdalene and the other Mary went to see the tomb. And suddenly there was a great earthquake; for an angel of the Lord, descending from heaven, came and rolled back the stone and sat on it. (28:1-2)

… the angel said to the women, "Do not be afraid; I know that you are looking for Jesus who was crucified. He is not here; for he has been raised, as he said. …* 'He has been raised from the dead, and indeed he is going ahead of you to Galilee; there you will see him.' This is my message for you." (28:5-7)

In Galilee, the place of the promised sighting, the disciples encountered the risen Jesus as the angel had promised. But this did not happen on either of the great historic Jewish mountains— Mount Moriah or Mount Sinai. It was just "a mountain" in Galilee,

---

* There is a small section (28:9-10) that tells of an encounter between the two Marys and the risen Jesus. It was almost certainly added to Matthew a century after the gospel was originally written. This is partly believed because its placement at this point in the text disrupts the gospel's otherwise seamless narrative. When this section is omitted, and the gospel returned to the original, Jesus appears only once, on an unnamed "mount in Galilee."

significantly unnamed. Matthew, once again, is explicitly rejecting the Temple Mount in Jerusalem. The new mountain of the Messiah is not in a particular place. It is anywhere, and everywhere. It is within.

Since there is only one, single appearance of the risen Christ in Matthew's gospel, he clearly wishes his entire gospel to end focused upon the points he makes here. And the words he chooses are a reiteration and expansion of the prophet Daniel's revolutionary vision—the same one that Jesus referenced in his trial before Pilate. These final words defy the foundation of Jewish belief. When the resurrected Jesus appeared in Galilee to his disciples, he decisively announced that the full power and unity of both heaven and earth were his, and his alone. He claimed all divine and temporal authority. He spoke in the name of the One God, and he gave a command that must have completely astounded his listeners.

Jesus the Messiah, the risen Christ, told the disciples to leave the mountain, taking its power, God's power, with them. He instructed them to take the power of God, the inner power they had gained, and what they had learned, out to every place and everyone. He instructed them to teach discipleship—the process of intimate relationship with Spirit they had learned from him—to one and all, near and far. He directed them to share the lessons of love, to tell others that the divine has only one source, and that every person is a son and daughter of that source.

Antiochian Jews must have found this instruction not only revolutionary but horrifying. They were Jews. They trusted, in an understanding as deep as their history, that the God to whom they prayed was uniquely their God, not everyone's. God's covenant with Abraham had made them first among all people, specially privileged. The Jewish Messiah had come—and of course he had come for them alone. It must have been almost impossible for them to believe that after two thousand years of Jewish suffering, hoping and waiting, they were not going to receive any exceptional acknowledgment.

Jesus' instruction told them their centuries of expectation were unfounded, and that they must completely renounce the privilege they believed was theirs. Even further—they must give their privilege away to "all nations," even to the oppressors! It must have seemed impossible—almost absurd. After all, their world already felt as though it was rocking with theological earthquakes, and the logical course in an earthquake is to hold on to what is solid, not to let it go. How could their precious Messiah ask them to give up the belief in their privilege when they had already lost so much? It must have been a deeply dismaying challenge for the suffering Messiahians.

The direct and simple beauty of the last line of the gospel must have allayed the dismay and confusion, however. With the same full power and authority of heaven and earth with which he gave his difficult instructions, Jesus the Messiah pronounced, "Remember." He told his followers never to forget—that they were not alone, that he was with them, loving them, "to the end of the age." This is, indeed, the fitting and final message to which Matthew has brought everything in his gospel.

Now the eleven disciples went to Galilee, to the mountain to which Jesus had directed them. When they saw him, they worshiped him; but some doubted. And Jesus came and said to them, "All authority in heaven and on earth has been given to me. Go therefore and make disciples of all nations...* and teaching them to obey everything that I have commanded you. And remember, I am with you always, to the end of the age." (28:16-20)

———— ∞ ————

When we consider how this last section of Matthew's gospel resonates within our own lives, we might first be tempted to think

---

* Present day Bibles include the phrase "baptizing them in the name of the Father, and of the Son and of the Holy Spirit" at this point in the text. This phrase is commonly referred to as 'the baptismal commission' and was added to the gospel some hundred years after the original text was written. We know this because the concepts of Father, Son and Spirit did not crystallize until after full separation from Judaism had occurred and self-identification of early followers as 'Christian' had commenced.

in terms of how dissimilar our experience is today. After all, we know that in the Mediterranean basin, as in most parts of the world, early human groupings were tribal. Each village had their own God, and their beliefs determined their entire understanding of the world. Indeed, tribal culture still dominates in many places. The essentially tribal fears and trepidation of Antioch relate more to us than we might realize. The idea of something larger and more cooperative than the tribe, a "nation state," is really very recent in the history of humankind.

You may recall from earlier in this book my description of the sense of "village" I learned from my Lebanese family. I was taught that we only "knew" people from our village, even if we could see the villages of outsiders in the distance. These tribal understandings shaped my early development and I now understand they were, in many ways, similar to those of many Americans in rural areas and large, urban neighborhoods.

Today, most of us no longer live this way, and we have told ourselves that our understanding is different and more "sophisticated." Yet we still retain many vestiges of the old patterns. We find ourselves suspicious of those who differ from us in ways large and small. We keep company with those most like ourselves, and we speak of outsiders as "them"—in our families, our work, our churches, our countries.

So while the fearfulness of Jesus' command may have lessened somewhat over the centuries, its basic challenge has not. The words are still inspiring, and their practice is still daunting, no matter how much we may believe in the principle of oneness. We are, after all, on the first path.

The self-assurance we have begun to gain on our trek up Matthew's mountain has given us a glimpse into our next challenge, the stormy sea. Throughout Matthew we have been called—like Joseph, husband and dreamer—to accept emotional exile, and make an original journey. To accomplish this, as Joseph did, we have had to put our usual sense of knowing aside and begin walking to an inner voice. In these last lines of Matthew, we begin to realize, as Joseph did, that the cost to heed this inner voice will be enormous.

At the beginning of his gospel, Matthew recounted the story of the Messiah's lineage and the coming of a child to be named *Emmanuel*, which means "God is with us." The last line of the Gospel of Matthew has given us the power to continue and sustain our journey. It is the unequivocal promise: "Remember, I am with you always, to the end of the age."

This is the answer to all of our questions and all of our fears. The earthquake we are feeling is also opening the tombs for our saints to arise. They are with us. God is with us. Now we are headed for Rome and the very stormy sea of the Gospel of Mark. We will carry Matthew's final message as a staff, holding it dear as we stride toward the waves that glint before us. The second path, and its gospel, will be another great challenge, but I promise you that we will make our way through it. Remember—there is not just one gospel. Nor are there two gospels, or even three. There are four gospels in the journey of quadratos. We can, and will, traverse the second path—and the third—and the fourth. We have the map. Do not forget. We are not alone. We are never alone. With God's promise in our hearts, let us move into Mark's gospel.

Prayer for the First Path
Psalm 121

I lift my eyes to the mountain peak –
Where does my help come from?

It comes from you
Maker of heaven and earth
Who holds my foot firm on the path up
Who's constantly present
Everywhere aware

Look!
With you there's no obscurity
Nothing is dim, asleep, inert
To those who question and struggle
You respond, keep hold, give cover
So that by day the sun won't burn
Nor by night the moon mesmerize

You guard against evil
Enfold and reveal the soul
Guard my arrival
Secure my departure–
Now:

Always

—translation by Norman Fischer

Exercises for the First Path

Create Temenos

Temenos is a Greek term which literally means "to make a cut or furrow in the ground." It was particularly used to indicate the unbroken cut that marked off the area where a temple was to be built, and the unbroken cut was intended to assuage fear that the protection offered by divinity might escape. The Greeks understood that to go to a temple was risky behavior. One went to a temple to ask a question, and asking meant that one did not know, a very frightening admission to the ego. The ego therefore required some sense of safety to make the journey into the unknown. The gods offered the needed wisdom, and temenos assured one's safety with the gods in the temple.

In our present-day world, I regard temenos as a very useful way of understanding the balance between feeling safe and taking risk. Too much safety easily leads to complacency, as we slip into the illusion that safety and security are our prerogatives. The opposite is equally true. Too much risk, and overload is often the result. Overstimulated, overwhelmed, we choose the opposite illusion and decide the journey is just too painful, and beyond our capacity.

The practice of the first path is a continual discovery of the balance between inspiring ourselves to the truth that we *must* journey, and avoiding those people and inner places where we become paralyzed and give up beginning, or continuing the journey.

Therefore: find and gather the words, people and stories that enable trust and inspire movement or the desire for movement.

Find: a Trusted Advisor, Spiritual Guide, or Mentor

Begin: a Daily Practice of Reflection, Meditation and Prayer

Gather: Stories and Films that inspire—that remind you that this journey has been made by others.

Welcome the Heyoka

The Lakota people of North America have a concept called the *heyoka*, or "the other." A person identified as a heyoka, whether male or female, becomes an official "opposite," feeling and thinking and expressing what others will not. The heyoka dresses in heavy clothes in the summer and lightweight fabrics in the winter, walks backwards, laughs when others are sad and is sad when others are happy. Their most important role is served when the people are in deliberation at council. As a decision begins to gain approval, the heyoka must speak loudly and strongly to the opposite opinion. The Lakota believe that every voice and every position on an issue must be given a respectful hearing before the people can make a correct discernment. Heyoka is a specific name from a specific people, but this practice of offering respect to every voice and position is generally found throughout the indigenous people of the Americas.

Listen for the annoying, irritating opinion inside yourself, amongst your family members, your friends, your region or country. Though uncomfortable, make a promise to try to respectfully entertain *all* positions, especially those that you would normally reject automatically. Attempting to welcome these ideas does not mean following them—but it does mean getting to know them, and trying to understand those who do hold these differing positions. Each of these may hold the key to your next step—or even your entire journey.

As We Leave the Mountain
Reference and Reflection

The great, overarching message of Matthew is trust and courage. In writing to the early Messiahians, who didn't even know they were to become founders of a new religion, his steadying words still echo with prophetic insight and pragmatic counsel invaluable to all who are on the first path of quadratos. How often are we, too, surprised by the completely unexpected way events turn out in our lives?

The genealogy of Matthew, the story of Joseph, the arrival of the magi and the baptism of Jesus tell us to search not only our individual histories, but the experience and stories of others for inspiration. Every great example we find reminds us that arduous journeys can be accomplished—and that they are worthwhile. Remain open to surprise. Great gifts come from seemingly improper, contradictory or uncomfortable sources. And above all else, remember, God is with us. Even when ash falls from the sky, or waters rise, we are beloved.

Herod's example, Mary and Joseph's return to Egypt and the devil's temptations ask us to learn from our fears over making a new journey, and confront them. When we return to a place of deep wounding, enter and abide there. Spirit will loosen its hold and lead us to larger freedom. We need to discipline ourselves to disregard "what if?" and "should have" and "if only."

The Beatitudes give us standards to emulate, goals to choose, and beautiful words to pray. We will be well served to keep them close at hand.

The Passion account affirms that if we truly accept the invitation to the journey offered by Jesus the Christ, we will stay "awake" to the entire process. Through prayer and self-reflection, we will have the inner resources to drink whatever cup is offered with a steady heart and mind.

The Resurrection account tells us that we must take personal responsibility for our spiritual lives and accept the challenge to make an original journey, while at the same time renouncing any self-righteousness or sense of being special that we may feel because of our "charge." Regardless of any inner or outer trials we encounter, we will always know that we are accompanied; that we have been promised, "…remember, I AM with you always, to the end of the age." Now, go!

CHAPTER FOUR

The Second Path: Crossing Mark's Stormy Sea

I am not asking you
to take this wilderness from me,
to remove this place of starkness
where I come to know
the wildness within me,
where I learn to call the names
of the ravenous beasts
that pace inside me,
to finger the brambles
that snake through my veins,
to taste the thirst
that tugs at my tongue.

But send me
tough angels,
sweet wine,
strong bread:
just enough.

—Jan L. Richardson

Endurance: Hope and Keep Going

THE SECOND PATH is without a doubt the most agonizing of the four paths—so it is a very good thing that it is also the least complicated, and tends to be the shortest. In the first path, we chose to thrust ourselves directly back into our greatest fears and insecurities, and now, in the second path, they fight back. It is a time of great discovery, but our revelations happen in an environment of terrific emotional and spiritual trial.

We feel as though we are in a small boat on a stormy sea—terrified, exhausted, fragile. The winds and water lash us as we are tossed about, in a gray, horizonless, directionless world. Is help coming? There is no way to tell, and in any case, we are not sure how to discern what would help and what would harm us further. We are thirsty, but only salt water surrounds us. Doubt fills us and it feels like the deepest failure. We feel pretty certain we will die.

We know we can't return to the beginning. At this point, we probably could not even find that place—but we don't really wish to anyway. We want to get through this time. Therefore, we have only one hope, and that is to fall back on ancient and proven practice. We pray. We stay attentive for a hopeful internal voice—a navigational star, a neighborly sailor who knows the waters better than we. We pray more. Then we follow the instructions we receive without question. We pray still more. We surrender again. And we continue to pray. It is precisely this bleak condition in which the early Christians of Rome in the middle of the first century found themselves—lost, alone, struggling to have hope. The Gospel of Mark was written as a compassionate beacon to light the way through their continued journey of faith, and it now illuminates our second path.

Birthplace of the Gospel of Mark: Rome, Mid-60s First Century

In the first century, Rome was the great Mediterranean center of power. Anyone who wanted to gain power or exert influence, or just wanted to be in the middle of things, had to go to Rome. By the year 60, Rome numbered some two million people, thirty to forty-thousand of whom were Jews. Though only two percent of the population, the Roman government paid a significant amount of attention to this minority, and thereby sustained a long-established pattern of discord and contention. Roman Jews would live in relative peace for a time. Then a problem would arise, and they would be evicted. They would return, enjoy a bit of peace, and then endure another eviction. This cycle occurred in 139 BCE, and again in 19 and 49 CE.

In the year 41, Emperor Claudius came to power. He immediately restricted the Jews by prohibiting the use of public places for worship, which effectively shut down the synagogues. The Jews regrouped and began using private homes as gathering places for Sabbath worship and other Jewish feasts and celebrations.

Everything remained quiet on the surface until the year 49, when rioting broke out in the Jewish quarter. Lacking any definite historical evidence regarding the cause for the riots, we do know that tension had been mounting in the Jewish quarter between traditional Jews and Messianic Jews who believed in the Christus (the Christ). We know that the Messianic Jews were accused of disturbing the peace and that Claudius responded to the disturbance by decreeing the expulsion of all Jews from Rome.

After Claudius died and Nero became emperor in the year 54, the Jews were allowed to return again. The apostles Peter and Paul, the two most prominent figures of first century Christianity, both lived in Rome during those mid-century years. Peter may have initially come in the 40s, been evicted and returned in 54. Paul is thought to have arrived sometime between 56 and 60. We do know, for certain, that in the agonizing years of the Gospel of Mark, they both lived in Rome—almost certainly in close proximity to each other in the Jewish quarter, a marshy area across the Tiber River from the hills on which the aristocracy resided in elevated splendor.

The Christian Church was ultimately to be founded on the differing gifts of these two powerful leaders, but their approaches were so dissimilar that conflict between them was inevitable. By all accounts, until coming to Rome, they had successfully avoided each other for years. Now they found themselves in the same city. Both were members of a troubled minority, in a time of great tumult, at the center of power. Their personal and theological differences stood in stark contrast as each vied for influence and loyalties in the Jewish community. It is strange irony indeed that the Christian Church later gave them a shared feast day—June 29th is the Feast of Saints Peter and Paul.

Peter was a laborer, possibly a fisherman, who grew up in Galilee, far from Jerusalem and its perceived high culture. He had known Jesus personally, been one of the inner circle of disciples, and was the titular (and cautious) leader of the Messianic Jews. Although we have almost no writings by Peter beyond two possible letters in the New Testament, tradition has frequently described his personality with words such as "gentle" and "accepting."

By contrast, Paul was a scholar and orator, who produced an extensive body of writings. They are the first and oldest Christian writings we have, dating from approximately 45 CE to 60 CE, prior to the first gospel. Although he grew up in Turkey, he was well-educated and very much at ease in Greco-Roman culture. Paul had a fiery heart and tongue, and had carried the message of the Christ across Asia Minor and Greece as a committed evangelist, although he had never personally known the historical Jesus. Accused of being a dangerous radical and enemy of the Emperor, Paul—unlike Peter—was a Roman citizen.

On July 19 in the year 64, an immense fire erupted in Rome. It blazed for five days, stilled, then ignited again for another forty-eight hours. The flames marched through most of Rome, and when the conflagration finally ended, most of the city lay in embers—not even the stately hillside homes of the aristocracy were spared. Many died. Common gossip spread among the devastated Romans that said Emperor Nero was responsible for the fire—that he had started it so that his proposals to raze buildings and rebuild Rome in a grand, classical architectural style could proceed unhindered. The tales proliferated, and Nero soon found himself under fire from his senators. He needed to find the real culprits, or at least someone to blame—and he needed to do it quickly.

Fate and ghetto geography provided his answer. The Jewish Quarter, untouched by the fire, made the Jews perfect scapegoats for Nero. The fact that the Jewish section was far away, across the river and on the outskirts of Rome (which is why it did not burn) was ignored. Word raced through the Quarter that the Jews were about to become Nero's way out of his predicament. Feelings re-surfaced from the earlier riot and expulsion in 49. Fear and anxiety rose and became near panic. The Jews had only been back in Rome for ten short years. Understandably, they dreaded another eviction, and feared the likelihood of even worse punishments exacted by the desperate emperor. Predictions of mass suffering and executions spiraled out of control.

Desperate to forestall what they were certain would be Nero's terrible wrath, a small group went to the emperor and confessed that a fringe group of Jews had indeed set the fire. They identified the culprits as the Messianic Jews, the Christus followers. Centuries later, it is impossible for us to know precisely what anxieties or divisions drove them to Nero with this story or what they expected that Nero would do. Today, we only know what Nero's horrific response actually was.

Nero immediately demanded that the Jewish community collaborate with Roman soldiers to identify those who belonged to the Christus group. Presented with a completely untenable situation and trying to reduce casualties, the Jewish community agreed to do so. What ensued was a mini-holocaust in the Quarter. Roman soldiers knocked on every door of the Quarter demanding to know if anyone in the house was a Christ believer. The householder's answer determined his fate and that of everyone else in the house.

If a believer was identified, either by others in the community or his own admission, the entire household was seized and publicly executed. The normal execution involved leading victims to the floor of the Circus Maximus, shackling them, splattering them with blood and then loosing starving dogs to eat them as Roman citizens watched. Today, twenty centuries later, when we visit St. Peter's Basilica and walk on its great Piazza or watch televised ceremonies held there, it is difficult to imagine that this was a place of terrible torture and slaughter.

If the head of the household denied being a believer, he was nonetheless required to name someone who was. There was no exemption from horror. The named individual was then summarily arrested and executed, with no opportunity for appeal or protest. Neighbor was forced to turn on neighbor. The number of executions mounted. Self-preservation became the order of the day. Family members even reported on other family members. Fear and paranoia reigned.

In the end, the Roman Christus community was totally destroyed. Among its many casualties were those of the great leaders, Peter and Paul. Although Peter initially fled Rome to avoid the holocaust, accounts written several centuries later told that his escape was stopped—not by Romans, but by a vision of the Christ. As the story goes, Christ appeared and asked, "Peter, where are you going?" Chastened, his conscience and faith reawakened, Peter reversed his footsteps and returned to Rome where he was immediately arrested and executed. Later, unsubstantiated accounts relate that he died after being lashed upside down on a post, or cross.

Paul had been charged as an enemy of the emperor, and travelled to Rome as a prisoner awating trial. As a Roman citizen, he was permitted to live under house-arrest, and had languished this way for at least four years. As a self-avowed leader of the Christus community, now a trial was no longer needed. Yet Paul would not meet death at the Circus Maximus. Every Roman citizen was entitled to the dignity of a "quick" execution and could not be tortured. Subsequent reports tell that he was beheaded. This is partly why many statues and paintings of Paul show him holding a sword. Other purported leaders of the Christus group were set afire and used as human torches for Nero's debauched banquets for the aristocracy.

What could possibly have been worse for the believers in the Christ? They identified themselves as faithful Jews, not Christians. (Self-identification as Christians would not come for another twenty years.) Their community had totally betrayed and abandoned them. Their families, their children, their elders—even Peter and Paul—had been gruesomely murdered. We can only imagine the overwhelming extent of their isolation and pain, and undoubtedly there must have been times when the promise of the Christ, the prophesied Messiah, seemed hollow and empty. Terror, shame, abandonment and death form the context of the Gospel of Mark.

Approaching Mark Today: Adrift in the Storm

While Matthew and Mark's accounts share many of the same historical elements, they shape their stories for their own communities in strikingly different ways. They each use distinct writing styles and metaphors, entirely changing the meaning of their narratives. Matthew expanded upon Mark's first (and therefore oldest) account. Many of their mutual themes, as well as the themes of the first and second spiritual paths we are exploring, overlap. If we look at them together, we can see that they are the gospels of beginning a journey, or a new journey, in faith. Later, we will see that the Gospels of John and Luke are quite different—from these, and from each other.

Not only is the Gospel of Mark the earliest written, it is the shortest of the four gospels. Correspondingly, the narrative of this gospel will be the shortest in Books One and Two. This brevity does not imply that Mark, or the second path of quadratos for that matter, hold any less importance than the other three. In fact, its concision has deep significance. Mark and the second path both house our most complex feelings—our fears, our resentments and our early wounds. Indeed, were we to spend too much time annotating and examining this particular path, we would likely defeat, or at least conceal, its unique power and gift. We might easily fall into masochism, perversely relishing the struggle and elevating it beyond its place as part of a greater process. Therefore, as we move through the gospel, be content with its brevity.

Although Mark's gospel was the earliest gospel written, the annual reading cycle of the Christian Church placed it second. And this completely matches our experience in the second path of quadratos. This path will offer knocks on the doors of our hearts, and some of them will be as fearsome as those in Rome millennia ago. The way in which we will choose to answer these knocks is the profound question we meet in this part of our journey.

As we proceed through the gospel, we will have very little poetry for company. Mark's language is terse and spare. He gives us nothing but the barest outlines. He does not paint the landscape with flowery descriptions. His stories are stark and revelatory. Why? First, because he was addressing Rome's Messianic Jews, who lived under a death sentence. They had no use for hearts and flowers. Second, because the core message of the gospel itself is simple, direct—even tough. That message is embodied, in this gospel, by a Messiah who fully understands the suffering of his followers—who came to earth, took human form and withstood agonizing pain. This Messiah wanted those who followed him to know that while their pain was necessary—because they were part of a much larger process—the Messiah not only genuinely understood their suffering but was there, in their very midst, as they suffered. And Mark didn't need a lot of words to do it.

Nonetheless, we will encounter some significant literary devices. Mark uses the metaphors of "wilderness," as well as two equivalent metaphors of wilderness drawn from Jewish history and tradition: deserts and bodies of water. Jews had to enter and traverse the Red Sea—the great barrier to their freedom, their nemesis—to escape Egypt. Seas in general were treacherous, wild and unruly places. In Hebrew writings, seas, lakes and rivers represent deep anxiety and even death, as does the desert. Myriad stories tell of the forty-year desert trial of the Jewish people, from which few survived to enter the Promised Land. Mark uses all of these to fill his gospel with compassion for the inner landscape of uncharted territory.

Despite Mark's often-bleak language, he does not—ever—deliver a singular message of difficulty. Nor does he depict trials that lead only into despair. We will see that he couples each image of wilderness with another image of comfort or hope. John the Baptist eats both locusts (yuck!) and wild honey. Sin is confessed and Holy Spirit is received. Heaven is torn apart and a dove descends. When Jesus goes into the wilderness he finds both beasts and angels. The bareness of his language may make this difficult to grasp at first, especially because our first impression is anything but hopeful. Mark gives us nothing but the barest outlines. There are no long descriptions; he fails to even list the temptations or acknowledge the angels with little more than a nod. Patience and close reading, though, will reveal the pairings.

As we enter this next stage of quadratos—the deep chaos of the second path and our own stormy sea—this straightforward style will give us comfort. We will find that it will suit the needs of the place we are in, and the ways we are able to hear. And Mark's specific words, through the four principal parts of his gospel, will illuminate, expand and guide us through this difficult part of our journey.

What Good News? Beginning the Gospel

Mark's gospel begins with a call to fill hearts with hope and gather strength. Clearly inspired, he announces "Good News!" Yet Rome's Messianic Jews didn't have much to celebrate. Even though they and their families had, as asked, professed Jesus as Messiah, their faithful obedience to His call resulted in their senseless slaughter.

"*What* good news?" they might well have asked. Yet, with his opening words, Mark insists that those hearing this text cast off all doubt. He reminds them of their most central belief, and calls them to the glory and joy it holds—the glory and joy that summoned them to believe in the first place. From this point of beginning, Mark will carry the Christus followers into the deepest understanding of their beliefs, and the possibilities of meaning and truth that lie within their great suffering.

The beginning of the good news of Jesus the Christ, the Son of God. (1:1)

One of the most startling differences between this gospel and that of Matthew is the complete absence of any kind of birth narrative, or indeed, anything about Jesus' early life at all. Mark moves immediately to one of the most powerful, persuasive and meaningful parts of the story of the Messiah for his audience—the account of John the Baptist and Jesus' baptism. Mark says that Jesus has arrived, and with nothing intervening, starts to recount the specific events he knows will matter most to the Messianic Jews in Rome.

To open the baptism narrative, Mark significantly calls attention to the prophesy of the "messenger" who was foretold by Isaiah in the 8th century BCE, as the coming of a Messiah who would suffer with his people. Mark also makes his first of eight separate references to the metaphor of "wilderness" in this initial twelve-verse passage.

As it is written in the prophet Isaiah, "See, I am sending my messen-ger ahead of you, who will prepare your way...the voice of one crying out in the wilderness: 'Prepare the way of the lord, make the lord's paths straight.'"(1:1-3)

At the Jordan River, multitudes answered John the Baptist's invi-tation to be baptized, just as they did in Matthew's gospel. But this is a very different baptism than Matthew's. While John the Baptist called for repentance in both gospels, in Matthew his call was directed to the Temple officials and privileged classes. Mark, with a different audience and objective, creates a completely different atmosphere. There is no mention of officials in this baptismal scene. Instead, Mark's multitudes are "people" who arrived at the Jordan to be baptized and confess their "sins." In this context, how does Mark intend the word "sin?"

Shunned by the larger Jewish community, the Roman

Messianic Jews carried great burdens of shame. And through the divisions within their faith community and Nero's executions, they had both seen and experienced the most brutal realities of human behavior. They harbored terrible feelings of disappointment and anger that ate at their inner lives and contaminated all of their relationships. These were the "sins" that Mark is calling on them to confess through the vehicle of John's mass baptism at the Jordan. He is showing them a way to release their pain and begin a process of forgiveness— forgiveness of themselves, of their families and of their community— so that they might move forward, and once again live full lives.

John the baptizer appeared in the wilderness, proclaiming a baptism of repentance for the forgiveness of sins. And people from the whole Judean countryside and all the people of Jerusalem were going out to him, and were baptized by him in the river Jordan, confessing their sins. (1:4-5)

John next announced that Jesus himself would soon arrive at the Jordan to baptize those gathered—and not just "with water, but...with the Holy Spirit." The message was clear, to the multitudes and to the Roman Messiahians. Confession had been made and the initial barrier of unresolved inner burdens removed. "Sin" had been cleansed. Now was the time to receive a baptism of "spirit," through Jesus the Christ. Now Spirit could truly enter.

John proclaimed, "The one who is more powerful than I is coming after me; I am not worthy to stoop down and untie the thong of his sandals. I have baptized you with water, but he will baptize you with the Holy Spirit." (1:7-8)

In the following verses, we read several of the juxtapositions mentioned previously. All are written in Mark's typically stringent language. Each begins with an image of great challenge, and ends with an image of promise. Through them, Mark assures the Messiahians that with every trial comes hope, which has, at its core, the truth that God remains with them in their suffering and will not abandon them. They call believers to use the words of the gospel in a practical way to transcend despair. Implicitly, Mark charges "Read on!" and "Read again!"

Notice the structure of these consecutive verses. These couplings—their apposed concepts, their sequence, their one by one narration and their stripped-down words—give the sense of a litany, or mantra. When we realize that first century Messianic Jews probably did not read these words, but rather prayed them aloud, often over and over, we can begin to grasp their beauty and effectiveness. There are many more passages like these in Mark's gospel—some before these and others that follow.

In those days Jesus came from Nazareth of Galilee and was baptized by John in the Jordan. And just as he was coming up out of the water, he saw the heavens torn apart and the Spirit descending like a dove on him. And a voice came from heaven, "You are my Son, the Beloved; with you I am well pleased." (1:9-11)

And the Spirit immediately drove Jesus out into the wilderness. He was in the wilderness forty days, tempted by Satan; and Jesus was with the wild beasts; and the angels waited on him. (1:12-13)

Now after John was arrested, Jesus came to Galilee, proclaiming the good news of God, and saying, "The time is fulfilled, and the kingdom of God has come near; repent, and believe in the good news." (1:14-15)

Our increased awareness of inner opposites and the connections between them will define the second path of our spiritual journey. Mark's juxtapositions typify many of the divisions we now feel. We started out hoping to gain larger life, more meaning and more vitality—or at least to jettison the worst of our problems. We entered the process knowing it would be difficult. We followed the instructions in this book: we found heroes and heroines, we created safe space, we sought wise advice, we opened ourselves as best we could, we meditated and prayed. But so far, it seems that everything we have done has been unavailing. We often feel disheartened as we approach the heart of the second path because the first path has left us in such a state of confusion. With more questions than answers we experience increasing despair and weariness.

I give you fair warning and fair promise: the real stripping is about to begin. This peeling of layers, this shedding of old beliefs, habits and assumptions, is absolutely necessary. Patience must become our core practice and we must recognize that "mindless" strength is its underpinning. Our brains will not help us in this place. We are beginning the process of what psychology calls "ego death." Mystics and shamans describe it as dismemberment, as being torn apart, limb from limb. In this time, psychologically, in all practical ways, we are still unborn. Our *belief* in new life, not its experience, gives us legs to keep walking.

Many of us try to shorten the process at this point, finding it just too painful. We feel that the sooner we return to the "light," the better. Frequently, our struggling ego-self rushes to forgiveness. Having visited the painful parts of our personal histories, we understandably choose to end our work on our past, and "decide" to start to view troublesome people, or events, with loving equanimity. These efforts initially seem positive and successful—especially when we receive praise and support for our "forgiveness" and "changed attitudes"—but, realize that these are mere surface adjustments.

The deep river of anger and fear still runs within us, no matter how far we try to submerge it under a facade of loving words. Our work does not end until we thoroughly strip ourselves to the core of our pain and anger and fear. Before we can truly alter these feelings, we must embrace and fully experience them with sufficient patience, for sufficient time.

If, however, we choose to stay in this uncomfortable place, and use the quadratos sequence of the gospels as a guide, we will see how the baptism in Mark's account builds on the instruction given in Matthew's. Having left our old ways, we must now confess our "sins." Gradually, we learn that confession is not a recounting of unearned shame. It has nothing to do with the relentless inner punishment we exact from ourselves when someone betrays us, or we fall short of unjust parental or social expectations. Rather, confession requires us to scrutinize our inner life, partially so that we may, once and for all, rid ourselves of the debilitating shame.

In twelve step programs, making "a searching and fearless (inner) inventory of ourselves" constitutes the fourth step. This is precisely what we must do now. As much as we would like to avoid this process, we must become aware of our limitations, our inner pain and the transgressions of both ourselves and of others. At the same time, we must accept the equally significant challenge to identify our strengths, our gifts and our good deeds. In this manner, we will also begin to better develop the ability to hear, know and accept the clarity of our own inner voice.

As we take responsibility for our transgressions we also need to assume "appropriate" guilt—the recognition of fully understanding and accepting our wrongdoing—and then express our genuine desire for forgiveness when that is possible. When at all possible, we make restitution, taking care to do so in a self-compassionate way. While we rigorously strive for self-honesty, we must also agree to grant ourselves the same understanding and latitude that we freely grant to others.

Taking responsibility also requires us to acknowledge "inappropriate guilt"—a deeper issue of addressing the shame we may hold, resulting from our instinct to blame ourselves for burdens which are not truly ours. They can result from emotional or physical neglect, physical, sexual or psychological abuse. They are most often things we internalized as children, usually placed upon us by society or our parents, often unknowingly, sometimes not. Whatever they are, if we are doing our deepest journeying, the second path is where we will discover their deadly impact on our lives—and where we must stop and take the steps toward healing them, if we are to continue our spiritual quest. In this instance, the second path can become much more lengthy.

We cannot do this alone. Much of this "inner inventory" we will be able to take by ourselves. And when we have done so, and begin to achieve sincere understanding through it, we must also stand humbly before another human being and fully, honestly and voluntarily share ourselves with them. Once we reach this difficult, poignant and wondrous point, and open ourselves to being truly known, we can begin the process of fundamental change. We can truly absorb and accept help and wisdom. Finally, we can begin to actually release our pain. These steps of inner repair are the "sins" and the "repentance" of the Gospel of Mark.

If we have more serious burdens of shame, such as those caused by childhood neglect and abuse, then we will need further help. We cannot turn away from this necessity. Our solitary perspective, even in prayer, will not be sufficient to move us through these difficult passages. Counselors who are specially trained in the work of re-processing early childhood development or groups such as Adult Children of Alcoholics/Trauma are the resources we must seek out.

Yet, no matter what the level of confusion or pain we uncover, it is important to remember that our suffering is temporary—and we have chosen to bare ourselves. We have done this because we know it is necessary to clearly reveal the Christ within, to touch love.

Confusion and Discernment: On and Around the Sea of Galilee

Mark's next set of lessons uses topography, alternating his narratives between the wilds of the desert south of Jerusalem and the terrors of the Sea of Galilee. Skillfully using this geography, he presents the trials of paradox and offers the real promise of a living path through their rigors and confusion.

Maintaining the theme of geography, even the physical aspects of Jesus' spiritual practice are deftly woven into the next verses. With the same constant cadence of the tide in the sea of Galilee, Jesus prayed, then went out; returned to pray, then went out again. He was baptized (prayed) and then driven out into the desert. He sought solitude to pray, then returned to minister to the crowds. He both circled and crossed the sea. Mark uses this pattern to reinforce some of his wisest counsel: "Amidst confusion," he advises, "amidst the demands of others and one's internal clamoring, stop. Leave. Go to prayer. The true course is found in a quiet, centered heart."

In the morning, while it was still very dark, Jesus got up and went out to a deserted place, and there he prayed. And Simon and his companions hunted for Jesus. When they found him, they said to him, "Everyone is searching for you." Jesus answered, "Let us go on to the neighboring towns, so that I may proclaim the message there also; for that is what I came out to do." And he went throughout Galilee, proclaiming the message in their synagogues and casting out demons. (1:35-39)

From chapters two through eight, Mark continues his narrative by describing Jesus' ten-city tour, historically known as the Decalogue (in Greek, literally, "ten cities"). As Jesus encircled the shores of the Sea of Galilee, he made no less than four crossings with his disciples. The accounts of these crossings hold the core teachings of this gospel.

The dramatic first crossing account exemplifies all four accounts. The Messiah demanded that the crossing take place at night, making it all the more terrifying and incomprehensible. A great storm arose, leaving the disciples trapped in a small boat tossing in the dark, unable to see, knowing only that their lives were in imminent danger. What did Jesus do in the midst of this terror and chaos? He slept peacefully in the rear of the boat on a cushion, while his disciples rushed around in panic. At last, in despair, they roused him and pleaded that he rescue them: "Teacher, do you not care that we are perishing?"

The hysteria felt by the disciples in the boat paralleled the emotional state of the Roman Messianic Jews. Stranded by their faith in the Messiah and assailed on all sides, their lives, too, were in peril. Like the disciples, they were very, very frightened. We can almost hear their anguished queries: "Has the Messiah really come? Is he with us? Has God abandoned us?" Mark's inspired message assured them that the Christ was with them, just as he had been with the disciples in the storm-tossed boat.

In the raging storm, once the disciples begged in fear, Jesus' voice called out: "Be still!" and immediately, the storms stopped. Awed by Jesus' omnipotence, the disciples accepted the evidence of this divinity within their individual hearts and minds, discussed it among themselves, and immediately rushed to deify him. Similarly, in each of the other crossing stories, when Jesus commanded, any and all turmoil ceased. These demonstrations of divine power and authority not only amazed and comforted the disciples, they also reassured Rome's Messianic Jews. Jesus was the savior they needed in their hour of trial! He pronounced loudly and restored order. He *was* the all-powerful Messiah. He would protect them. They had no reason to fear death!

However, as the gospel progresses, it becomes apparent that this is not Mark's complete message at all. In the ensuing three crossing stories, Mark recounts that Jesus grew increasingly impatient with the presumptions of his disciples that he would simply perform a divine act and in every instance relieve them of their fear. They seemed to completely ignore that they had responsibilities also. Their obligation was to endure and to find inner calm through faith. By the final crossing, Jesus was totally exasperated and demanded to know if his disciples had yet learned anything whatsoever.

The disciples still sought a God who rescued them, who removed obstacles. They wanted to remain safe—as children— with a God who acted as an all-powerful, protective parent. They could not yet fathom a God who not only did not do this, but who actually pushed his followers into dark, nighttime storms. They did not yet have the spiritual maturity from which they could derive inner equilibrium and serenity. They had not yet discovered an inner place of God.

On that day, when evening had come, Jesus said to them, "Let us go across to the other side." And leaving the crowd behind, they took Jesus with them in the boat, just as he was. Other boats were with him. A great windstorm arose, and the waves beat into the boat, so that the boat was already being swamped. But Jesus was in the stern, asleep on the cushion; and they woke him up and said to him, "Teacher, do you not care we are perishing?" He woke up and rebuked the wind, and said to the sea, "Peace! Be still!" Then the wind ceased, and there was a dead calm. Jesus said to them, "Why are you afraid? Have you still no faith?" And they were filled with great awe and said to one another, "Who then is this, that even the wind and the sea obey him?" (4: 35-41)

"Do you still not perceive or understand? Are your hearts hardened? Do you have eyes, and fail to see? Do you have ears, and fail to hear? And do you not remember?"(8:17-18)

※

Uncertainty, depression and anxiety run rampant along this second path. We teeter on the cliffside edge of chaos. But we must jump off that cliff. Like Jesus' followers, we are called to step out in faith and make a fearful journey through the conflict of opposites for the sake of our souls. Like the disciples, our frightened hearts call out: "Fix it! Fix me! Show me the strength I was promised. Use it on my behalf—please, please!" We remember the first path of Matthew fondly—at least we could make out the top of the mountain—even if the path was rocky and difficult. We pray that someone—or something—will arrive to dispel the fear in our hearts, subdue our panic.

Sometimes, we do receive reassurances in our trials, and we clutch them joyfully. They take many forms—the glow of a promising new relationship, a new teacher with "real" wisdom, the perfect job—and provide comfort. Those who "think like us" may give us consolation but these seeming answers are not likely to become permanent solutions. Our real challenge becomes that of discernment. How do we know what is true? How do we decide what to keep—and what to throw away?

The simple, unadorned maxims of twelve step programs often seem appropriate to this time. Developed for people caught in dismal circumstances, who are determined to escape without resorting to old patterns, they provide clear tools for coping with paradox. Note how well the effortless simplicity and beauty of the well-known "Serenity Prayer" captures the essence of Mark and the second path:

God, grant me
the serenity to accept the things I cannot change,
the courage to change the things I can,
and the wisdom to know the difference.

We must describe—encircle—the inner places that hold our chaos and conflicts, inner and outer, in the same way that Jesus circled the Sea of Galilee. Gathering our courage, we then need to walk directly into them and pray. We will learn the deepest, most important lessons in the tempests of our own stormy seas, and emerge ready to engage in proper action—action born not of ego, but of the Christ within.

Although the Gospel of Mark doesn't have much joy, it does have a continuing and resounding message of strength and faith. Despite all the differences in the crossing accounts, the core truth remains the same: the Christ is always with us. This truth must constitute the foundation of our daily spiritual practice, as we strive to stay in trust. As we grip the gunwales of the small boat of our humanity, we can never forget that we are never alone. Even if we are blinded — whether by avoidance or fear or pain; even if we make mistakes;

even if we feel abandoned, tossed to the heavens at one moment and to the depths at the next—we will never be alone.

—⟨⟩—

Teachings about Power: Caesarea Philippi, The Transfiguration and the Journey to Jerusalem

In this chapter, Jesus and his disciples have moved to the northern foothills of Caesarea Philippi, known today as Israel's boundary with Lebanon and Syria. In the first century, this region was known for the natural spring that flowed from these mountains into the Sea of Galilee and on to the Jordan River, where it finally emptied into the Dead Sea. Again, Mark artfully uses topography to make his point.

As the source waters rushed downhill to become a river and sea, they increased in size and danger. Similarly, as Jesus and the disciples followed their route from the spring to the Sea of Galilee, then down to the Jordan River valley, and finally into Jerusalem, they walked in increasing danger, proceeding directly to Jesus' crucifixion. Mark dramatically juxtaposes the cities of Caesarea Philippi and Jerusalem: overflowing birth joined to imminent death.

On the way to the source waters, Jesus asked his followers a daunting question: "Who do you say that I am?" One by one they answered, but Mark focuses on Peter's response. "You are the Messiah," he answered. Mark goes on to detail how Jesus then ordered his disciples to keep his divinity confidential, seemingly a strange request. But Jesus didn't give this instruction out of a need for secrecy or of a sense of modesty or shame, but rather from love. He knew his disciples still lacked the maturity to understand all the complexities and implications of "Messiah," much less the full path of true discipleship. He therefore used both his question and Peter's answer as the prelude to a great teaching.

First, Jesus recounted the series of events he knew to be imminent—his suffering, rejection, death and resurrection. Upset,

Peter began to rebuke Jesus for his prediction. Abruptly, Jesus snapped at him: "Get behind me Satan! For you are setting your mind not on divine things, but on human things." Peter's reaction proved that he was still "young" in his faith. Peter had become accustomed to thinking of the Messiah as a wonder-worker, with the power to banish every difficulty. He assumed Jesus could and would save himself from death. His conception demonstrated his shallow understanding of the real nature of power, and of the Messiah, and serves as a message from Mark to the Messiahians in Rome: "If you are looking for a miracle-working Messiah, then you have not yet understood the nature of your faith."

Jesus then addressed the true path of discipleship. He told those gathered that if they wanted to follow him, they would experience great trial and conflict. They could not avoid, evade or divert their fate, nor could they count their cost. They could only accept and endure. Finally, he promised them that if they did this, if they followed the path, they would come to know God. This inspired central message was specifically directed at the Messiahians, who regarded Peter as the founder of their community, and as a great hero who would have died for his faith. Mark's account reassured them that even Peter's immature faith had wavered.

Jesus went on with his disciples to the villages of Caesarea Philippi; and on the way he asked his disciples, "Who do people say that I am?" And they answered him, "John the Baptist; and others, Elijah; and still others, one of the prophets." Jesus asked them, "But who do you say that I am?" Peter answered him, "You are the Messiah." And Jesus sternly ordered them not to tell anyone about him. Then Jesus began to teach them that the Son of Man must undergo great suffering, and be rejected by the elders, the chief priests and the scribes, and be killed, and after three days rise again. He said all this quite openly. And Peter took Jesus aside and began to rebuke him. But turning and looking at his disciples, Jesus rebuked Peter and said, "Get behind me Satan! For you are setting your mind not on divine things but on human things." Jesus called the crowd with his disciples, and said to them, "If any want to become my

followers, let them deny themselves, take up their cross and follow me.
For those who want to save their life will lose it, and those who lose their
life for my sake, and for the sake of the gospel, will save it. For what will
it profit them to gain the whole world and forfeit their life?" (8:27-36)

Six days after the teaching at Caesarea Philippi, Jesus took three disciples to a high mountain where they witnessed him "transfigured." As their Messiah appeared even nobler, more holy and beautiful, the three looked on in amazement as the great Hebrew figures of Moses and Elijah appeared and were seen talking with Jesus. The sequence from Caesarea Philippi to the Mount of Transfiguration recalls the creation account in the first chapter of Genesis. On the first day, the spirit of God hovered over the waters. And on the sixth day, man and woman, differing yet complementary realities, were created in the image of God. Mark's text re-states the sixth day with the differing yet complementary realities of Moses and Elijah. In Jewish tradition Moses stands for law, structure and discipline while Elijah represents mercy, compassion and crossing boundaries. Like male and female, Moses and Elijah are opposites that either fall into perpetual discord or gradually mature into a harmonious whole.

Mark uses this vision of Jesus the Christ, holding opposites together, to amplify Jesus' earlier message at the spring. This time, the disciples actually saw Jesus in the full glory of his divinity—yet again Jesus ordered them to conceal their knowledge. He knew they still did not comprehend the true nature of enduring conflict and, consequently, the true nature of divine glory. One opposite—Moses—is not to be chosen over another—Elijah. The Christ holds all opposites together. To achieve the great work of harmony is to patiently endure conflict until the true nature of divine glory is manifested.

Six days later, Jesus took with him Peter and James and John, and led
them up a high mountain apart, by themselves. And Jesus was transfig-
ured before them, and his clothes became dazzling white, such as no one

on earth could bleach them. And there appeared to them Elijah with Moses, who were talking with Jesus. Then Peter said to Jesus, "Rabbi, it is good for us to be here; let us make three dwellings, one for you, one for Moses, and one for Elijah." Peter did not know what to say, for they were terrified. Then a cloud overshadowed them, and from the cloud there came a voice, "This is my Son, the beloved, listen to him!" Suddenly when they looked around, they saw no one with them any more, but only Jesus. As they were coming down the mountain, Jesus ordered them to tell no one about what they had seen, until after the Son of Man had risen from the dead. So they kept the matter to themselves, questioning what this rising from the dead could mean. (9:2-10)

After descending the mountain, Jesus led his disciples away from Mark's metaphoric wilderness, the Sea of Galilee, and set out directly for Jerusalem. Every step they took towards the city led them closer to the painful end of their teacher's physical life. Along the way, Jesus never stopped teaching, though he knew that they would not understand many of the lessons he taught them until after they had witnessed his death and resurrection.

Over and over again, Mark reiterates his primary tenet: "Walking a path of faith is not only worthy, it is of greater value than life itself." He has Jesus shift his language to dreadful and horrific imagery, filled with severed limbs, ravaged flesh and the fires of hell. Unknown to the disciples, these descriptions helped to prepare them for the intense pain and conflict they would soon feel in their hearts, souls and minds. Two thousand years later, the psychological accuracy of these metaphorical descriptions is stunning.

Mark wanted to emphasize the depth of commitment required for the Messianic Romans to survive. In essence he demands that they must, in their prayers, ask for the very fire in which they will burn. He further insists that they will have to be "salted with fire," a reference not found in Matthew's gospel. Why?

In the first century, salt was more valuable than almost anything else—equal to gold. It could preserve meat, and therefore gave protection from starvation and illness. It protected against dehydration in the arid desert. It meant survival. Wars were launched and fought over it. In the Temple, only meat that had been treated with salt was offered. The Romans rubbed their infants' lips with salt to protect them against evil, and they also tied salt to the heads of those they executed, making the condemned an offering to the gods.

Those who believed Jesus was the Messiah were very likely to be executed—sacrificed in the arena—and were therefore likely to receive the precious salt. This is perhaps the most powerful paradox of Mark's gospel: salting as a sign of sacrificial death and also as a metaphor for the inestimable worth of God's love. When Messiahians heard: "Everyone will be salted with fire," they understood that they were receiving a promise and a blessing that would make their death worthwhile.

"If any of you put a stumbling block before one of these little ones who believe in me, it would be better for you if a great millstone were hung around your neck and you were thrown into the sea. If your hand causes you to stumble, cut if off; it is better for you to enter life maimed than to have two hands and to go to hell, to the unquenchable fire. And if your foot causes you to stumble, cut it off; it is better for you to enter life lame than to have two feet and to be thrown into hell. And if your eye causes you to stumble, tear it out; it is better for you to enter the kingdom of God with one eye than to have two eyes and to be thrown into hell, where their worm never dies, and the fire is never quenched.

For everyone will be salted with fire. Salt is good; but if salt has lost its saltiness, how can you season it? Have salt in yourselves, and be at peace with one another." (9:42-50)

The lessons that Jesus taught in Mark's crossing accounts and at Caesarea Philippi are some of the most challenging in all of the gospels to comprehend and adapt for our daily lives. They force us to purge our traditional conception of God as a super-parental divine rescuer. These lessons have a clear message: God is certainly capable of rescuing us, but God will not rescue us, because rescue will kill our journey. The journey is long and full. It contains peacefulness, joy and ecstasy, pain, paradox and conflict, all of which we must eventually learn to balance, in order to reach a capacity for inner serenity. This is the way of quadratos. This is the way of the Christ.

In this second path, it is as if we are in a tiny boat on a menacing sea. Ahead lies a far shore with a landscape we would not yet recognize, even if we could see it. If we are ever to make landfall, we must let go— give up all our attempts to steer the boat. Instead, we have to drop our sails, find our oars and row. And pray. We have to make a straight voyage of great strain and total surrender. We must not allow the demons in the depths below nor the thunder and lightning above to deter us.

Many of us will choose to stop right now, right here. Indeed, many of our wounded faith systems encourage us to do just that. They ask us to take a walk to the altar, light a candle, say a word and then remain as emotional and spiritual children in a bright and effortless glow. Stopping now, when we've barely started, dooms us to failure, for this is the place where we discover our level of commitment to the journey. This is where we acknowledge our true reliance on God's grace. We're tempted to stop, to negotiate, to make bargains to shorten or ease the burden of the inner work that must be done. One of the dangers of this path is our desire to choose one opposite over another. We cannot, must not, give in to this desire. It will lead unfailingly to a less-than-complete life in the less-than-satisfactory company of a less-than-perfect and mysterious god.

As we maneuver into the undulating sea of our fears (and their sources) everything shifts. Waves crush our old assumptions, smashing our past-held truths and behaviors, leaving us discomfited. We find ourselves constantly checking, and re-checking our every premise, calling, in effect, "Get thee behind me, Satan." Mark's gospel makes clear that when faced with adversity, our best ally is prayer. Jesus consistently brought his disciples back to some form of contemplating spirit. This practice enables us to experience suffering in a meaningful and expansive way.

When faced with pain and conflict, and left to our own limited resources, we tend to overuse our intellect. We attempt to think our way out of the dilemma, or we distract ourselves by arguing. These are narrow courses, driven by our fearful, threatened ego. However difficult, we must try to ignore that inner "chatter." We must pray for our necessary trials, rather than our rescue. Most importantly, we must accept and accept and accept some more, often without really understanding.

The second path of quadratos teaches that there is no true course except that which leads us to fully comprehend "losing life" to gain it. Through prayer and proven counsel, we learn to accept our trials and live with them, knowing that we cannot hasten or alleviate the rigors of the path itself. Every time we attempt to avoid a situation, we do little more than reduce our opportunity to grow, to learn from the journey. Like the immature disciples, looking for a God who merely provides or repairs, we are, in fact, asking God to become smaller with us. Fortunately, God is not so paltry. The Mystery will not be diminished; nor will it ever abandon us.

Mark pays particular attention to Peter. As we saw in chapter eight, Mark knows that the Roman Messiahians will best relate to Peter. He walked the path. He made the journey. He struggled. He suffered. He erred. But he survived his immaturity, endured and eventually arrived on the far shore. He discovered the landscape there and explored it well. He found peace and a full and vital life. He became a great hero of his faith. "Here is your proof," Mark says to Roman Jews, "Here is the life of a fallible human. It is possible. Let his example draw you forward."

This has two applications for us. One is the critical practice of self-compassion—absolutely vital as we make our inventory. Wisdom can only travel through error, difficult though that is. The other is a re-iteration of the counsel we received in Matthew—find help. However, in this case, it is a bit more specific. Peter is a mentor. He is someone who has traveled the path. In twelve-step parlance, he would be called a sponsor—someone who has made the journey successfully and can serve as a trusted spiritual guide, as a soul-friend. We need someone like this—a living example, and someone with whom we can share our travails, and whose advice we can trust.

Speaking the Truth: Confrontations in Jerusalem's Temple

After his long trek, Jesus finally arrived in Jerusalem. He went directly to the Temple, where a bustling scene of commerce confronted him. People buying and selling animals for sacrifice filled the room. The Temple system designated the "holiest" sacrifices as the most expensive—but even the most modest offerings bore exorbitant prices. Jesus, outraged over the extortionate system, which forced humble petitioners into corrupt practice, unhesitatingly began over-turning tables and pronounced that the Temple was no longer a "house of prayer" but a "den of robbers." Recognizing a direct threat to their authority, the priests and scribes immediately started to talk of murdering the charismatic and contentious interloper.

Mark knows that the Christus community is in direct opposition to the leaders of synagogues in Rome. He wants to fortify his audience with the example of the Messiah he shows here—confident, forceful, walking directly into conflict. Mark wants to encourage the Roman Jews and give them the strength to "speak truth to power," regardless of what they might have to endure as a result.

Then they came to Jerusalem. And Jesus entered the temple and began to drive out those who were selling and those who were buying in the temple, and he overturned the tables of the money changers and the seats of those who sold doves; and he would not allow anyone to carry anything through the temple. He was teaching and saying, "Is it not written, 'My house shall be called a house of prayer for all the nations?' But you have made it a den of robbers." And when the chief priests and the scribes heard it, they kept looking for a way to kill him; for they were afraid of him, because the whole crowd was spellbound by his teaching. (11:15-18)

The following day, Jesus returned and directly confronted the Temple authorities. They argued, and tension mounted quickly as Jesus emphatically and clearly responded to their inquiries. He left, and then returned to Jerusalem, and the Temple, for a third time. This time he spoke in parables, each crafted for his Roman audience. One story told of heartrending conflict and loss endured by "a man who planted a vineyard." Nonetheless the man persisted and the parable closed with a reference to a "rejected stone" that became a "cornerstone." This parable, with its reference to planting, building and the vineyard that would produce new wine, was a powerful message to the Messianic Jews. "Persist," it said. "Even though you are cast aside, the vines will still be planted, and recognition of the Messiah will yet come. You are the cornerstone of the foundational changes in your faith. Your lives, your sacrifices, are not in vain."

Again they came to Jerusalem. As he was walking in the temple, the chief priests, the scribes, and the elders came to him and said, "By what authority are you doing these things? Who gave you this authority to do them?" Jesus said to them, "I will ask you one question; answer me, and I will tell you by what authority I do these things. Did the baptism of John come from heaven, or was it of human origin? Answer me." They argued with one another, "If we say, 'From heaven,' he will say, 'Why then did you not believe him?' But shall we say, 'Of human origin?'" they were afraid of the crowd, for all regarded John as truly a prophet. So they answered Jesus, "We do not know." And Jesus said to them, "Neither will I tell you by what authority I am doing these things." (11:27-33)

Then he began to speak to them in parables. "A man planted a vineyard, put a fence around it, dug a pit for the wine press, and built a watch-

tower; then he leased it to tenants and went to another country. When the season came, he sent a slave to the tenants to collect from them his share of the produce of the vineyard. But they seized him, and beat him, and sent him away empty-handed. And again he sent another slave to them; this one they beat over the head and insulted. Then he sent another, and that one they killed. And so it was with many others; some they beat, and others they killed. He had still one other, a beloved son. Finally he sent him to them, saying, 'They will respect my son.' But those tenants said to one another, 'This is the heir; come, let us kill him, and the inheritance will be ours.' So they seized him, killed him, and threw him out of the vineyard. What then will the owner of the vineyard do? He will come and destroy the tenants and give the vineyard to others. Have you not read this scripture: 'The stone that the builders rejected has become the cornerstone; this was the Lord's doing, and it is amazing in our eyes'?" When they realized that he had told this parable against them, they wanted to arrest him, but they feared the crowd. So they left him and went away. (12:1-12)

Mark's next chapter brings the conflict with the Temple authorities to an apocalyptic conclusion. Again, Jesus spoke in dramatic images, this time of destruction and re-birth. Mark wants the Messianians to understand the nature of fundamental change—and to understand that terrible conflict is one of the necessary and expected steps of all transformation. In the same way that Jesus the Christ died, but was resurrected—the mini-holocaust they were experiencing in Rome would not bring the end of their new faith. "This is how change works," Mark was teaching. "This is how strong foundations are built. You must clear out the old. There are always terrible struggles as the old paradigm fights back, then crumbles to make room for the new one that arises." These words gained even greater impact (and irony) to readers in subsequent decades because only a few years after Mark wrote his gospel, Jerusalem's Temple was leveled in Rome's great assault.

Jesus' final exhortation in this chapter was to "keep awake!" All three synoptic gospels—Matthew, Mark and Luke—use these words, but each

131

places them at a different point in the account, presumably to call specific attention to the matters of greatest import to each gospel author. Mark locates them directly at the close of the contentious debate with the Temple authorities and ensuing lessons on the nature of deep change—and immediately prior to the Passion account. He does this to be sure his audience remains awake and vigilant—and that they understand that there is no escape from necessary pain. It is part of the journey of Spirit.

"...When you hear of wars and rumors of wars, do not be alarmed; this must take place, but the end is still to come. For nation will rise against nation, and kingdom against kingdom; there will be earthquakes in various places; there will be famines. This is but the beginning of the birth pangs. As for yourselves, beware; for they will hand you over to councils; and you will be beaten in synagogues; and you will stand before governors and kings because of me, as a testimony to them. And the good news must first be proclaimed to all nations. When they bring you to trial and hand you over, do not worry beforehand about what you are to say; but say whatever is given you at that time, for it is not you who speak, but the Holy Spirit. Brother will betray brother to death, and a father his child, and children will rise against parents and have them put to death; and you will be hated by all because of my name. But the one who endures to the end will be saved." (13:7-13)

"Truly I tell you, this generation will not pass away until all these things have taken place. Heaven and earth will pass away, but my words will not pass away." (13:30-31)

"And what I say to you I say to all: Keep awake." (13:37)

⌘

Through the centuries, it has been easy for people to read Mark's words about apocalyptic happenings, look around their world, and take his words literally. But we are more interested in their universal patterns, particularly as they relate to quadratos. We do not need to prepare for external "end times." We need to transform our inner selves so that we will not cause or be party to the external events that lead to catastrophe. In our journey of inner transformation, Mark's gospel provides invaluable metaphors for the powerful feelings that we undergo in the second path, when death and destruction and collapse, dressed in depression and despair, surround us.

Our message today echoes Mark's message to believers in Rome long ago: "This is not at all the end, even though it feels as though it might be. You must expect inner and outer conflict, and the uncertainties that arise with such conflict. Try to remember that this is what it feels like when the deepest changes occur. Hold on. Hold on. Later, you will be able to see how unexpectedly the new cornerstone was chosen, and with what stability it was laid."

As we faithfully walk this path, our immature ego-self reluctantly gives way, as Spirit transforms us. Resistant to change, the immature ego fights back, just like the Temple authorities did, and it does so with great skill and determination. It may encourage us to make choices between opposites, rather than to patiently wait in the discomfort of conflict and paradox. We must recognize that necessary inner conflict can readily become outward conflict with others and that this is not the true course. It is the siren call of the ego-self attempting to re-take control from Spirit, luring us to the soul's slumber. We must "keep awake."

Staying Present: The Passion

In keeping with the rest of his gospel, Mark's Passion is the shortest found in the four accounts. Starkly and unsparingly, he weaves an emotional fabric of powerful conflict and the deepest, most painful abandonment. Written with the certain knowledge that many of the Christus followers would relate very directly to the feelings held within it, he knew that they would not simply "remember" the death it described, they would see their own deaths reflected in every word.

The Last Supper and the Garden

Mark's account of the Last Supper is particularly poignant. Jesus foresaw his betrayal by an intimate, someone "dipping into the same bowl," and he said so. Rome's Messianic Jews knew this also. When the centurion knocked on their door, they knew the betrayal had come from someone close to them. When they heard the words of the gospel, it was as though the Messiah himself was warning them not to betray each other, and not to betray the new community of the Son of Man.

After Jesus' meal with his disciples, the group went to the Mount of Olives. There, Jesus told his followers that even though only one would betray him, all of them would desert him. Peter protested, specifically reiterating the word "desert." As always, Mark chooses his words with extreme care. Matthew, less precise a wordsmith, uses the words "deny," "desert" and "betray" interchangeably in his gospel. Mark, however, has subtle distinctions for each of these.

In Mark's gospel, Jesus used the word "betray" to refer to those who totally gave up their belief, or, like Judas, turned someone else over to the authorities. He used the word "desertion"—which literally means to turn one's face in another direction—to describe those who gave into the impulse to avoid conflict. Something that, as Jesus predicted, everyone did.

It is likely that, by the time Mark wrote this gospel, the disciple Peter had already deserted Rome, returned and been killed for his faith. I believe that while Mark encouraged his audience not to flee like Peter, he was simultaneously extending great compassion. By focusing on Jesus' prediction that, given the circumstances, inevitably "all" would desert, Mark lets the Messianic community know that some might emotionally or physically *need* to flee. Both Jesus and Mark knew that the combination of young faith and terrible challenges could lead to a lapse in faith, in vigilance. They also knew that desertion, unlike betrayal, would not critically damage the soul—deserters could redeem themselves, turn around again and return to the path.

Mark also uses the word "denial" in this passage to connote the most modest level of abandonment. He uses "denial" as a claim of "not knowing"—even when one actually does—illustrated by Peter's denial of knowing Jesus. This choice of words tells the Christus community that even the most faithful of disciples can have momentary lapses and abandon their faith. But they can also immediately understand their error, repent and be restored.

Mark knew that before the knock on the door came in Rome, the Messiahians would have ample time to reflect. However, once the door opened and the centurion asked his question, they would have time for only one answer. Mark therefore wanted his audience to understand that, like the disciples, they had four choices, each of which held different spiritual and moral consequences. He used clear examples and clear language. "When you are asked: 'Are you a follower of the Christus?' you can: answer 'Yes.' Or, you can deny or desert or betray. Those are your four choices, and your only choices." Mark implores them to directly confront their belief, and to do so thoughtfully and deeply. Matthew's gospel, in contrast, rocks back and forth in a very different rhythm—a theme of betrayal and return, betrayal and return.

When it was evening, Jesus came with the twelve. And when they had taken their places and were eating, Jesus said, "Truly I tell you, one of you will betray me, one who is eating with me." They began to be distressed and to say to him one after another, "Surely, not I?" Jesus said to them, "It is one of the twelve, one who is dipping bread into the bowl with me. For the Son of Man goes as it is written of him, but woe to that one by whom the Son of Man is betrayed! It would have been better for that one not to have been born." (14:17-21)

When they had sung the hymn, they went out to the Mount of Olives. And Jesus said to them, "You will all become deserters; for it is written, 'I will strike the shepherd, and the sheep will be scattered.' But after I am raised up, I will go before you to Galilee." Peter said to him, "Even though all become deserters, I will not." Jesus said to him, "Truly I tell you, this day, this very night, before the cock crows twice, you will deny me three times." But Peter said vehemently, "Even though I must die with you, I will not deny you." And all of them said the same. (14:26-31)

Mark's account of Gethsemane follows the same spare and direct form as the rest of the gospel. It tells us that Jesus took with him the same three disciples who accompanied him at the Transfiguration—Peter, James and John. He requested that they stay awake with him in the garden in his time of grief and prayer. Since these were the three who had witnessed the transfiguration, one might assume that they would have taken these instructions with great seriousness. Nonetheless, they slept. Despite this disappointment, Mark, again, empathetically displays more compassion than Matthew for his audience, through Jesus' response to his failing disciples. We can also note that Peter remains Mark's focus, singled out for remonstrance (as opposed to all the disciples in Matthew). Finally, Mark has Jesus pray the central message of this gospel: O Mysterious God, even though You are omnipotent, please provide me with what You know to be best, even if it isn't what I want or yet understand.

They went out to a place called Gethsemane; and Jesus said to the disciples, "Sit here while I pray." Jesus took with him Peter and James and John, and began to be distressed and agitated. And Jesus said to them, "I am deeply grieved, even to death; remain here and keep awake." And going a little farther, Jesus threw himself on the ground and prayed that, if it were possible, the hour might pass from him. Jesus said, "Abba, Father, for you all things are possible; remove this cup from me; yet, not what I want, but what you want." He came and found them sleeping; and Jesus said to Peter, "Simon, are you asleep? Could you not keep awake and pray that you may not come into the time of trial; the spirit indeed is willing, but the flesh is weak." (14:32-38)

To Pilate and the Crucifixion

The scene then moves to Peter's denials, and again Mark makes a slight but very meaningful change from Matthew's account, in which Jesus said that Peter would deny him three times "before the cock crows." In Mark, Jesus said the thrice denial will happen "before the cock crows twice." But wouldn't Peter have remembered Jesus' words when he heard the cock crow the first time? This tiny detail intensifies the impression of Peter's helplessness in the face of his all-too-human fear. Even when reminded, he was unable to stop himself, unable to change course.

Well aware that Rome's genocide continued over a protracted period, Mark knew that no one who betrayed his neighbor or his friend had the excuse of surprise. They had plenty of time to consider an answer before the soldier's knock came, and Peter's example drives that reality home.

While Peter was below in the courtyard, one of the servant-girls of the high priest came by. When she saw Peter warming himself, she stared at him and said, "You also were with Jesus, the man from Nazareth." But Peter denied it, saying, "I do not know or understand what you are talking about." And Peter went out into the forecourt. Then the cock crowed. And the servant-girl on seeing him, began again to say to the bystanders, "This man is one of them." But again, Peter denied it. Then after a little while the bystanders again said to Peter, "Certainly you are one of them, for you are a Galilean." But Peter began to curse, and he swore an oath, "I do not know this man you are talking about." At that moment the cock crowed for the second time. Then Peter remembered that Jesus had said to him, "Before the cock crows twice, you will deny me three times." And Peter broke down and wept. (14:66-72)

The Passion account proceeds to Jesus' appearance before Pontius Pilate, where the parallels between Jerusalem and Rome continue. Pilate chose to ignore what he knew to be the truth about

Jesus and accepted the judgment of the "crowd," agreeing to Jesus' crucifixion. Nero, in scapegoating the Messianic Jews for the fire in Rome, had also abandoned truth and taken an expedient course. Mark intensifies the pain of these betrayals which moved beyond the private arena into the public.

Now at the festival Pilate used to release a prisoner for them, anyone for whom they asked. Now a man called Barabbas was in prison with the rebels who had committed murder during the insurrection. So the crowd came and began to ask Pilate to do for them according to his custom. Then Pilate answered them, "Do you want me to release for you the King of the Jews?" For he realized that it was out of jealousy that the chief priests had handed Jesus over. But the chief priests stirred up the crowd to have Pilate release Barabbas for them instead. Pilate spoke to them again, "Then what do you wish me to do with the man you call the King of the Jews?" They shouted back, "'Crucify him!" Pilate asked them, "Why, what evil has he done?" But they shouted all the more, "Crucify him." So Pilate, wishing to satisfy the crowd, released Barabbas for them, and after flogging Jesus, he handed him over to be crucified. (15:6-15)

After the trial, in the courtyard, Mark gives us a dramatic image: the soldiers strip Jesus and robe him in purple—a color reserved for royalty (and dramatically different from the red robe found in Matthew). They crown him with thorns, and abuse and mock him as "King of the Jews." The soldiers belong to Pilate. They defend and represent the temporal world, and cannot see past it. Mark uses the ugliness and childishness of this scene— and Jesus' lack of response to it—to illustrate the spiritual immaturity of the temporal world, and the Temple followers who had condemned Jesus.

When the time arrived to be led to his greatest physical trial, the crucifixion, the purple robe was removed. Jesus was described as being in "his own clothes." Spiritual power needed no outward trappings.

Then the soldiers led him into the courtyard of the palace (that is, the governor's headquarters); and they called together the whole cohort. And they clothed him in a purple cloak; and after twisting some thorns into a crown, they put it on him. And they began saluting him, "Hail, King of the Jews!" They struck his head with a reed, spat upon him, and knelt down in homage to him. After mocking him, they stripped him of the purple cloak and put his own clothes on him. Then they led him out to crucify him. (15:16-20)

Mark's brief depiction of the Passion contains no extra words, and few explanations. He does write that Simon of Cyrene, named as the "father of Alexander and Rufus," carried the cross for Jesus. It is possible that Alexander and Rufus were members of Rome's Messianic Jewish community. If true, this mention provides one more link to this community. Furthermore, if Alexander and Rufus accepted execution in Rome, their mention here would have provided further inspiration to the Christus followers. In an account with language as sparse as Mark's, their mention would seem to have some significance, but we can only conjecture.

They compelled a passer-by, who was coming in from the country, to carry Jesus' cross; it was Simon of Cyrene, the father of Alexander and Rufus. (15:21)

Jesus was led to Golgotha, stripped naked and crucified with two bandits. Contrary to what has often been thought, his stripping was not a special attempt to dishonor him. Nakedness was the norm for Roman executions, but it was extremely shameful for Jews, who considered public nudity a terrible disgrace. As Jesus hung on the cross, awaiting death, everyone taunted him: bystanders, the bandits, the chief priests and scribes. Finally, at three o'clock, six hours after being nailed to the cross, Jesus cried out the beginning words of Psalm 22: "Eloi, Eloi, lema sabachthani?" which means, "My God, my God, why have you forsaken me?" *(See Appendix B for the three major Aramaic/Hebrew variations of this line.)*

Mark's gospel records these as Jesus' only words—and through the millennia, they have been subject to myriad interpretations. Many have believed that Mark's Passion shows Jesus betrayed and consumed by feelings of despair, but I believe that this interpretation is not at all appropriate, correct or supported by the text itself. It would also be completely inconsistent with Mark's message to Rome.

In the first century, as we noted in Matthew, it would have been no aberration, nor any great surprise, for Jesus—or any Jew—to have recited the words of this particular psalm at the moment of their death. Jewish tradition called for a pious Jew to die with the words of Psalm 22 on his lips, and reciting the first words would have indicated the same thing as a Christian starting to pray, "Our Father... ." What we did not discuss in Matthew, however, is the nature of Psalm 22 itself, a psalm that every devout Jew would have known from beginning to end. This psalm is a prayer that does, indeed, begin in lament. However, it continues on to celebrate trust and faith in the midst of agony, and even death. If we understand that Jesus was *quoting* a great and triumphant prayer, a core piece of Hebrew scripture, it makes absolutely no sense to think of him sagging from the cross, bloody, abandoned and inconsolable.

In Mark's gospel, Jesus the Christ was indeed betrayed, and when he gave a "loud cry and breathed his last," he was certainly bloody and alone. Not a single one of his disciples are noted as having been around him when he died, including Mary, his mother, although it is mentioned that women including Mary of Magdala watched "from a distance." Mark gives no indication that Jesus surrendered to bitterness or despair. To the contrary, he calmly predicted his fate to his disciples; he calmly prayed for the hour in Gethsemane to pass so that he could continue to the events of his death. The shame and mockery heaped on him by the soldiers, and from every side as he hung on the cross, did not affect him. He refused the palliative wine offered him. Instead, Jesus prayed Psalm 22, calling on the most compassionate tradition of the Jewish people, with a full heart. There is no sadness in this account. Rather, at the very end, crying out, Jesus marshaled all his energy, all the strength of his belief, for a last, full moment of proclaiming God.

Mark's Passion is a remarkable and clearly inspired account of a physically excruciating death. Yet, from the time the soldiers seized Jesus the Christ after his encounter with Pilate, to the moment of Jesus' death, we read of no gesture, no movement or any word whatsoever from him. When, at the last moment of his life he does speak, with full awareness, he utters a glorious declaration of God's enduring love. Psalm 22 begins in lament, but goes on to proclaim God's glory, ending with the words: *"To God, indeed, shall all who sleep in the earth bow down; before him shall bow all who go down to the dust, and I shall live for him. Posterity will serve God; future generations will be told about the Lord, and proclaim the Lord's deliverance to a people, yet unborn, saying that God has done it."* (Psalm 22, verses 29-31) Mark's picture of this defining moment gave the Roman Jews the essence of the genuine power of the true Messiah.

After the death, Mark recounts that among the watching strangers and enemies, a centurion, upon seeing the serene and stately strength of Jesus, exclaimed, "Truly, this man was God's son!" How immensely meaningful these six words were! When the Messianic Jews went to be sacrificed in Rome, they too would face a centurion. Surrounded by strangers and enemies, shackled and dying, they would also be taunted. Mark called on them to understand that the manner of their death contained the seed of conversion residing in the power of great spiritual example and would proclaim the reality of Jesus the Christ that could be carried forward to generations.

Then they brought Jesus to the place called Golgotha (which means the place of a skull). And they offered him wine mixed with myrrh; but he did not take it. And they crucified him, and divided his clothes among them, casting lots to decide what each should take. It was nine o'clock in the morning when they crucified him. The inscription of the charge against him read, "The King of the Jews." And with him they crucified two bandits, one on his right and one on his left. Those who passed by derided him, shaking their heads and saying, "Aha! You who would destroy the temple and build it in three days, save yourself, and come down from the cross!" In the same way the chief priests, along with the scribes, were also mocking him among themselves and saying, "He saved others; he cannot save himself. Let the Messiah, the King of Israel, come down from the cross now, so that we may see and believe." Those who were crucified with him also taunted him. When it was noon, darkness came over the whole land until three in the afternoon. At three o'clock Jesus cried out with a loud voice, "Eloi, Eloi, lema sabachthani?" which means, "My God, my God, why have you forsaken me?" When some of the bystanders heard it, they said, "Listen, he is calling for Elijah." And someone ran, filled a sponge with sour wine, put it on a stick, and gave it to him to drink, saying, "Wait, let us see whether Elijah will come to take him down." Then Jesus gave a loud cry and breathed his last. And the curtain of the temple was torn in two, from top to bottom. Now when the centurion, who stood facing him, saw that in this way he breathed his last, he said, "Truly this man was God's Son!" There were also women looking on from a distance. Among them were Mary Magdalene, and Mary the mother of James the younger, and of Joses, and Salome. (15:22-40)

In this most difficult second spiritual path, we must hold tenaciously to the lessons of Jesus the Christ and the example of Peter we find in the Gospel of Mark. Through the actions of these two figures, more powerfully than through their words, we can gain counsel that can help us through this chaotic sea.

Aside from Jesus himself, Mark makes Peter the primary figure of this gospel, putting him in every chapter, except those describing the crucifixion and resurrection. Why? Because Peter was very much like us. He struggled to remain "awake." He faithfully followed all the steps. He was present, bodily and spiritually, at all of the important moments of the gospel. Despite all of his efforts, he literally fell asleep, he denied his Messiah and he was not present at the crucifixion. By any measure, he failed.

When Peter fell asleep, he did so at a critical moment. When he denied Jesus, he did so despite having been warned, and even in the face of a vivid reminder—the first cock's crow. Yet he did not stop himself. And then he cried. And then he disappears from the remainder of the gospel. We do not see him again. Why?

Peter represents a living, breathing historical example for Mark—one that includes large measures of paradox and uncertainty. Peter failed. He had great lapses of faith, but Mark knows, as did his audience, that Peter ultimately became a hero and died for his Messianic beliefs. Mark's message is that failure and guilt are redeemable, regardless of the number of lapses. Resolution, in turn, might take a very long time and be filled with uncertainty. So, spiritually and literarily, Peter's purpose ended the moment he shed his sincere tears of regret, but his usefulness to us as an echo of the second path is immeasurable: attentiveness, struggle, failure and no resolution.

The Serenity Prayer used in twelve-step programs (quoted earlier in the chapter) almost perfectly captures the essence of the Christ's lessons for us. In the first half of Mark's gospel, Jesus is presented with challenges he "knew he could change." He ascertained this through prayer which made him decisive and forceful. Over and over, Mark characterizes his response with the word, "immediately." In the Passion account, however, Jesus faced trials he knew he could not, and should not, change.

Therefore, in the Passion, with full understanding, Jesus the Christ embodies the deep and true power of surrender. He accepts. He stays centered, calm and dignified. He does not speak out, for there is nothing to say. His example conveys that there is nothing external that can or should be fought. His only battle is the same as ours in this second path—to stay awake, to stay connected to Mystery, and to use all of our energy to proclaim God's love, even in the midst of pain and conflict.

The Resurrection Announced

Mark's resurrection narrative is a puzzling, even startling, end to a profound gospel. It contains four elements that are completely unique to it—not contained in any of the other gospels.

After Jesus' burial, the same women who watched him die "from a distance" went to the tomb to anoint the body. They did this, not because they believed in resurrection, but because they wanted to be sure that Jesus' burial was in accordance with Jewish law.

When the women got to the tomb, they saw what Mark describes as a "young man dressed in a white robe." This is the first puzzlement. Although it has been assumed by many that this figure was an angel, Mark does not tell us this.

The young man presented the second surprise when he informed the women that Jesus had "been raised." He went on to issue instructions that the women inform the disciples of a meeting with the risen Christ. In the narrative that follows, though, clear to the end of the gospel itself, we read of no actual sighting. It isn't there. A century later, another ending was added that did contain a sighting, but the original gospel has none.

The instructions that the women were asked to relay to the disciples denoted a meeting with the risen Christ in *Galilee*. This is the third apparent oddity. In the first century, a reference to Galilee customarily referred to the entire region of the Sea of Galilee. Mark pointedly directs the disciples back to his metaphorical region of chaos and wilderness to see their risen Messiah.

I find the fourth enigma most interesting of all. The text says the women did not fulfill their instructions. Instead, they fled and *"said nothing"* to anyone. They were frightened. The word "afraid" is the final word of the gospel that Mark writes to the Roman Jewish community. Christian readers in subsequent years found this ending so unsettling that not only one, but two, more "satisfactory" endings were written in the second century. No one has ever been able to give a coherent, logical reason for Mark's inexplicable closing.

I believe the original ending is neither obscure nor some kind of odd lapse or digression on Mark's part. His gospel is extremely precise, pointed, accurate and consistent. I believe that the word "afraid" best resonated with the Messianic Jews of Rome to whom he wrote, as a direct challenge to them—a rhetorical question. It asked: "When the soldiers come to your door, I know you will be afraid. What will your answer be? Will you betray, or desert or deny? Or will you give witness to the Messiah?"

When the sabbath was over, Mary Magdalene, and Mary the mother of James, and Salome bought spices, so that they might go and anoint him. And very early on the first day of the week, when the sun had risen, they went to the tomb. They had been saying to one another, "Who will roll away the stone for us from the entrance to the tomb?" When they looked up, they saw that the stone, which was very large, had already been rolled back. As they entered the tomb, they saw a young man, dressed in a white robe, sitting on the right side; and they were alarmed. But he said to them, "Do not be alarmed; you are looking for Jesus of Nazareth, who was crucified. He has been raised; he is not here. Look, there is the place they laid him. But go, tell his disciples and Peter that he is going ahead of you to Galilee; there you will see him, just as he told you." So they went out and fled from the tomb, for terror and amazement had seized them; and they said nothing to anyone, for they were afraid. (16:2-8)

Mark's original—and perplexing—ending fits the second path of quadratos as precisely as it fit the Jews in Rome. It challenges us. Will we manage to endure our continuing fear of conflict and death, and also bear witness to a deeper reality? Will we betray "the way" and give up, amid all the temptation? Will we desert, turn our faces away and run? If we do, will we return? Will we accept one (or many) of the possible distractions and deny the path? If we do, how long will it take us to recover our direction? Will we ever recover? Or will we somehow manage to make our way through the uncertainty and confusion and follow the path we must, like Jesus did to Jerusalem?

The walk through this second path will not likely look as straight and true as that of Jesus to Jerusalem. Eventually, when we are more mature in our journey, and as we make more cycles of quadratos, it may straighten a bit, but now, at this early stage, we are much more like the disciples, like Peter. Jesus said they would "all" desert him—and they all did, despite their sincerity. We too will probably desert, in some way or another, but remember, as Peter showed us, desertion is a redeemable transgression.

Through this miserably uncomfortable process, we learn what it is that we "can change" and what we "cannot change." As we paddle across the sea of chaos, we will fall over the side of the boat and gulp a fair amount of seawater. We will get seasick. But as long as we keep praying—and rowing—we will not sink.

Indeed, the Christ promises us that the far shore will grow closer and closer. Awareness of the grace that guides us will begin to dawn, surely and certainly. The storms will quiet and land will appear. Our boat will slide smoothly onto the sand of a golden beach, and right over a rise, just behind the sea grass, the most beautiful and fragrant garden that we can possibly imagine awaits. John's glorious garden is preparing our welcome. In the shade of a bending tree, amongst the blossoms, we will find a bench, and we will see our name on it. Hold to faith; let our courage be blessed. We will soon rest.

Prayer for the Second Path
Psalm 22

My God, my God, why have you forsaken me?
Why so far from my delivery
So empty in the anguish of my words?
I call to you in the daytime but you don't answer
And all night long I plead restlessly, uselessly

I know your holiness, find it in the memorized praises
Uttered by those who've struggled with you
Through all the generations
These, my forebears, trusted you
And through their trusting you touched them
Held and delivered them
They cried out to you and you met them face to face
Their confidence was strong and they were not confounded

But I am not as they
Utterly alone, I am cast out of the circle
A worm, a living reproach, scorned and despised, even
less than despised
Unheard, unseen, unacknowledged, denied
And all who encounter me revile me with cynic laughter
Shaking their heads, parting their nattering lips, mocking
"Let him throw himself at God for his deliverance,"
they say
"Since that is who he trusts let the Lord save him."

And they are right:
How not to trust you, and what else to trust?

You I entered on leaving the womb
You I drank at my mother's breast

I was cast upon you at birth
And even before birth I swam in you, my heart's darkness

Be not far from me now
When suffering is very near
And there is no help
And I am beset all around by threatening powers
The bulls of Bashan gaping their dismal braying mouths
Their ravenous roaring lion mouths

I am poured out like water
My bones' joints are snapped like twigs
My heart melts like wax
Flooding my bowels with searing viscid emotion
My strength is dried up like a potsherd
My tongue cleaves woolly to the roof of my mouth
And I feel my body dissolving into death's dusts

For I am hounded by my isolation
Am cast off and encircled by the assembly of the violent
Who like vicious dogs snap at my hands and feet
I count the bones of my naked body
As the mongrels shift and stare and circle
They divide my clothes among themselves, casting lots for them

So now in this very place I call on you
There is no one left
Do not be far from me
Be the center
Of the center
Of the circle
Be the strength of that center

The power of the absence that is the center

Deliver my life from the killing sharpnesses
Deliver my soul from the feverish dogs
Save me from the lion mouths
Answer me with the voice of the ram's horn

And I will seek and form and repeat your name among my kinsmen
In the midst of everyone I will compose praises with my lips
And those who enter your awesomeness through my words will also praise
All the seed of Jacob will glorify you
And live in awe of you
All those who question and struggle
Will dawn with your light
For they will know
You have not scorned the poor and despised
Nor recoiled disgusted from their faces
From them your spark has never been hidden
And when they cried out in their misery
You heard and answered and ennobled them
And it is the astonishment of this that I will praise in the Great Assembly
Making deep vows in the presence of those who know your heart
Know that in you the meek eat and are satisfied
And all who seek and struggle find the tongue to praise
Saying to you:

May your heart live forever
May all the ends of the earth remember and return to you
And all the families of all the nations bow before you
For all that is is your domain
Your flame kindles all that lives and breathes
And you are the motive force of all activity
The yearning of the grasses, the lovers' ardor
And they that rise up, live, and eat the fat of the earth will bow before you
Before you will bow all those who lie down, find peace, and enter the dust
For none can keep alive by his own power—you alone light the soul

Distant ages to come shall serve you, shall be related to you in future times
Those people not yet born
Will sing of your uprightness, your evenness, your brightness
To a people not yet born that is still yet to come
That this is how you are.

—translation by Norman Fischer

Exercises for the Second Path

The exercises of quadratos are cumulative. On the second path, we continue the practices of temenos and heyoka. These are present through all four paths. They are particularly essential on the second path, where we often feel exhausted, conflicted and anxious. Remember, this is transformation. We are moving through a type of death—and it is very difficult.

Hold the Tension of the Opposites

Christianity provides a powerful image of this practice. The tradition's earliest form of the cross was a simple "+" drawn with four equidistant arms. This is the form of the cross known and venerated in the first century. When we hear Jesus say in Mark, "pick up your cross and follow," it was this image he meant. The cross is a symbol of the joining of all opposites—left to right, and up to down. Indeed, if the symbol is laid flat, or turned in a circle, even those distinctions disappear. When you meditate or pray, see the simple + mark in your mind, or find an equidistant cross and keep it by you.

In prayer and in practice with others, listen to all perspectives and sides. Try to find truth in each and every one, no matter how opposed you feel initially. Know that in your sincere attempt to find truth you will discover great interior conflicts. Resist every tendency to take one side over another. Understand and examine the fact that the tendency to choose *any* one side at the expense of its opposite is an ego defense that serves no purpose except to make us feel better in the moment. The ego feels calm because it has something definite to latch onto—no uncertainty, no dilemma, no shades of grey, no anxiety. But this tendency is extremely harmful, almost by definition. Human interaction is complex and, if it is to be approached maturely, can almost never be judged with the kind of simplistic exactitude that soothes the ego.

The practice of the second path is to begin learning new kinds of responses to our dilemmas and questions. Our new ways of resolution will not insist that things are either/or, that we set things into conflict or that we make a choice of one thing over another. Our new ways will teach us that it is possible to find an answer that is both/and, that we can combine disparate elements of truth in a creative way and a new truth will appear. This new truth will be more expansive and it will serve both points of view instead of putting things into conflict. Of course, this new way requires that we learn the capacity to find truth in competing opposites—both of them, or even all of them.

And when we do, through prayer and spiritual practice, an even greater truth will be revealed that goes still further—that folds the opposites together. But we are not yet there. On this second path, our challenge is to endure and learn from the opposites—intensely listening to all sides, choosing neither. Holding the tension of opposites is our necessary trial as we hold true to the journey, hoping and believing in a new epiphany.

Ask to be Deepened

The lyrical poetry of Psalm 22 holds great mystery, grace and wisdom. It is possible that a time of deepest abandonment can open within us feelings of hope, and even praise.

A Buddhist prayer before meditation recites: "I pray that I may be given the appropriate difficulties and sufferings on this journey so that my heart may become awakened, and my practice of compassion and liberation for all beings may be fulfilled."

Vaclav Havel has said: "Hope is not the conviction that something will turn out well, but the certainty that something makes sense, regardless of how it turns out."

This age has enormous troubles. All ages have enormous troubles. We are not likely to ever know a completely trouble-free time in our life or in our world. Our practice in the midst of great concern, pain and emotional deprivation is to pray that the meaning in these moments will be made clear to us, and that we will have the courage to live the answer that the meaning provides.

As We Make Landfall
Reference and Reflection

Good News! The Gospel of Mark opens with the hopeful reassurance that our trials actually represent good news—a further opening of our spiritual journey. The message of the second path is hope and steadfast endurance through all obstacles!

John the Baptist calls us to "repent": scrutinize our lives, recognize the core source of our pain, acknowledge appropriate guilt, ask forgiveness, and then move on.

The storms at sea ask us to remember that we are not alone in the boat. They also tell us to listen for our inner "Rescue me! Fix me!" voice. When we hear it, we can know that this is a temptation to fall into feelings of being victimized. Mark asks us to respond with our greatest inner strength and determination to keep going, without losing compassion for ourselves and our frailties.

The Transfiguration advises us to be mindful of our lack of understanding. This path is largely a time of waiting in the felt tension between opposing figures and thoughts and feelings, and praying for the heart of Christ, and learning more before we speak or act.

The teachings on the road to Jerusalem tell us that we are on a deep and mysterious journey of transformation that cannot be made on our own. It will often be filled with pain and will feel completely incomprehensible. As we walk it, the help of Spirit will be essential.

The confrontations in the Temple tell us to take courage and to walk directly into our inner conflicts. The tension is necessary and inevitable as the old ego-self tries to wrestle control away from Spirit.

Jesus' teaching about apocalypse cautions us that when we find ourselves wanting to point fingers—externalizing our conflicts onto others—our practice is instead to focus on the transformation of our own inner lives.

Mark's Passion account tells us to look to the example of Peter, and the example of the Christ. Peter's story tells us we can expect to fall into denial or even desertion and that resolution may not come any time soon. Jesus the Christ shows us the power of surrender and the insignificance of anything except our connection with God.

The Resurrection asks us a significant question: what will our response be when we are challenged to step out in faith—especially when the cost is discomfort or turmoil or fear unto death? In the second path, it seems that almost every moment holds this question.

CHAPTER FIVE

Preparing for the Second Half of the Journey

WE BEGAN OUR journey climbing Matthew's Great Mountain covered in ashes from our temples lost. Then we moved to crossing Mark's Stormy Sea. The Gospel of Mark is a difficult way to end this book—particularly since it closes the first half of the journey and has the task of drawing us onward. Mark gave us no inspiring prose, no hearts and flowers to help us feel good as we concluded his gospel. The message was "hope and endure," with only the promise that matters would improve at some unknown, future time. Furthermore, the second path is surely the most exhausting of all the paths of the spiritual journey, leaving us emotionally adrift in a tiny boat, tossed by a tempest. I can completely understand if you feel that I am abandoning you in the midst of the worst possible circumstances. Yet my choice to end here is purposeful.

Some of us, and particularly those of us who are Christian, have likely felt some familiarity with the sequence we have traveled to this point. The idea that a spiritual journey begins with trial and inner examination is a long standing, three-step model in Christianity. Normally in that model, fulfillment would be the next stage—reward and result for the tribulation. But that is not the case with the quadratos pattern.

We have, indeed, taken serious steps of self-examination in the first and second paths, accompanied by the Gospels of Matthew and Mark. Mountain crags, wild storms and impenetrable wilderness have not stopped us. We began, we have persevered, and we definitely look to be affirmed for the seriousness of our intention and our commitment up to this point. But if quadratos is not the usual model, if result and reward are not what comes next, then what does? Why should we keep going? What will we find in the second half of the journey?

Book Two opens with the third path of quadratos. It is in the third path, particularly the latter part of the third path, where quadratos significantly diverges from the more familiar three-step model. Our companion for this path will be the Gospel of John, which has been responsible for some of the greatest ecstasy, as well as the most horrendous abuses, of the Christian faith. We will luxuriate in the glorious words of John's prologue, which open us to divine union in a deeply mystical way, completely different from any of the other gospels. We will study the profound metaphors within John and learn how the third path holds surprising and often demanding challenges. We will also examine the tragedy created by the literal interpretations of this gospel and, specifically, the age-old distortions of the words found in John 3, which have caused tens of thousands, even millions, of deaths.

Next, in a further departure from the three-step model, our journey will move to the Gospel of Luke, and the fourth path of quadratos. In this path, we will discover, not an end to our journey, but a place of perpetual new beginnings. We will reap the results and rewards we seek, but we will learn they are not a static prize, or a destination. Rather, they are an ongoing series of revelations in an increasingly intimate relationship with Spirit. With Luke's gospel, we will learn to successfully express these truths through pragmatic actions in our everyday lives. We will discover that a harmonious life with others requires neither completely open arms nor a stringently guarded heart. We will learn ways to be flexible, welcoming and wise.

In the final section of Book Two, we will discuss spiritual practices that I believe are necessary to move Christianity forward so it can meet the needs of yearning hearts in a complex world. Some of these practices are also applicable to other institutions— religious and psychological and cultural. I believe we must escape the focus on "three-ness" and move to a four-fold model of spiritual and psychological progression as quickly as possible. If we do not, and if our leaders continue to advise believers and patients and citizens to end their journeys before the end of the third path, those leaders will be co-responsible for the havoc in inner lives, and chaos in the world.

As long as we continue to live in the model of three-ness, we will be trapped in a world of the immature ego, and that emotional terrain will dictate everything—individual lives, religion, politics, and all institutions. Immature egos are always threatened and seeking to protect themselves; "right" and "wrong" can never find a place to meet; compromise or creative solutions are never options. It is often true that our spiritual, and even civil, leaders will not make the changes we need until we insist that they do so, on our behalf. I firmly believe that we need the model of quadratos in the world, and we need it now. If our leaders will not show us "the way," we must walk it until they are transformed.

The final blessing that an intentional journey through quadratos gives us is an increased ability to cope with change. We come to understand that change is necessary and inevitable. More importantly, we learn how to discriminate between change that is in the service of expansion, consonant with universal truths, and change that is not useful, that, instead, serves to contract us. A bit of peace arrives as we stop seeing ourselves as uni-dimensional and unchanging, and the world as a huge onslaught against which we must fight. We are able to truly welcome change.

Quadratos shows us that what appears as chaos is actually the boisterous and messy face of the new—not a sign of breakdown, but rather a sign of development, movement in a positive direction. Once we can welcome chaos as a face of change, we also can welcome an "outsider." Our ancient form of tribe welcomed individuals who looked or thought alike and condemned all others. Today, we must move beyond to form inner and outer communities where all are welcome, and diverse parts make a whole. In Book Two, we will see how the revered name, Jeru-Shalom—Jerusalem, holds a practice to move all of us forward.

We are always in process, and we are always meeting others in process. The journey of quadratos will help us accept the ongoing challenges of learning how to live with compassion, discrimination and Spirit. The entrances to our inner and outer communities will no longer be kept blockaded—or carelessly left open. Instead, we will craft intentional gates for ourselves that we will be able to open and close appropriately. This is the result of the full four-fold universal spiritual journey. This is the truth revealed by "the way" of Jesus the Christ, experienced in the sequence Matthew and Mark and John and Luke. This is the fullness of what lies ahead.

APPENDIX A

Sunday and Feast Day Gospel Reading Cycle
Roman Catholic

Sunday or Holy Day	1st Year or Year A	2nd Year or Year B	3rd Year or Year C
1st Sunday of Advent	Mt 24:37-44	Mk 13:33-37	Lk 21:25-28, 34-36
2nd Sunday of Advent	Mt 3:1-12	Mk 1:1-18	Lk 3:1-6
3rd Sunday of Advent	Mt 11:2-11	Jn 1:6-8,19-28	Lk 3:10-18
4th Sunday of Advent	Mt 1:18-24	Lk 1:26-38	Lk 1:39-45
Christmas Vigil	Mt 1:1-25	Mt 1:1-25	Mt 1:1-25
Christmas-Midnight	Lk 2:1-14	Lk 2:1-14	Lk 2:1-14
Christmas-Dawn	Lk 2:15-20	Lk 2:15-20	Lk 2:15-20
Christmas-During Day	Jn 1:1-18	Jn 1:1-18	Jn 1:1-18
Sunday After Christmas (Holy Family)	Mt 2:13-15, 19-23	Lk 2:22-40	Lk 2:41-52
January 1, (Solemnity of Mary, Mother of God)	Lk 2:16-21	Lk 2:16-21	Lk 2:16-21
2nd Sunday After Christmas	Jn 1:1-18	Jn 1:1-18	Jn 1:1-18
Epiphany	Mt 2:1-12	Mt 2:1-12	Mt 2:1-12
Sunday After Epiphany (Baptism of the Lord)	Mt 3:13-17	Mk 1:6b-11	Lk 3:15-16, 21-22
Ash Wednesday	Mt 6:1-6, 16-18	Mt 6:1-16, 16-18	Mt 6:1-6, 16-18

1st Sunday of Lent	Mt 4:1-11	Mk 1:12-15	Lk 4:1-13
2nd Sunday of Lent	Mt 17:1-9	Mk 9:2-10	Lk 9:28b-36
3rd Sunday of Lent	Jn 4:5-42	Jn 2:13-25	Lk 13:1-9
4th Sunday of Lent	Jn 9:1-41	Jn 3:14-21	Lk 15:1-3, 11-32
5th Sunday of Lent	Jn 11:1-45	Jn 12:20-33	Jn 8:1-11
Passion Sunday (Palm Sunday)	Mt 26:14–27:66	Mk 14:1–15:47	Lk 22:14–23:56
Holy Thursday- Chrism Mass	Lk 4:16-21	Lk 4:16-21	Lk 4:16-21
Holy Thursday- Mass of Lord's Supper	Jn 13:1-15	Jn 13:1-15	Jn 13:1-15
Good Friday	Jn 18:1–19:42	Jn 18:1–19:42	Jn 18:1–19:42
Easter Vigil	Mt 28:1-10	Mk 16:1-8	Lk 24:1-12
Easter Sunday-Day	Jn 20:1-9 or Mt 28:1-10	Jn 20:1-9 or Mk 16:1-8	Jn 20:1-9 or Lk 24:1-12
Easter Sunday-Evening	Lk 24:13-35	Lk 24:13-35	Lk 24:13-35
2nd Sunday of Easter	Jn 20:19-31	Jn 20:19-31	Jn 20:19-31
3rd Sunday of Easter	Lk 24:13-35	Lk 24:35-48	Jn 21:1-19
4th Sunday of Easter	Jn 10:1-10	Jn 10:11-18	Jn 10:27-30
5th Sunday of Easter	Jn 14:1-12	Jn 15:1-8	Jn 13:31-33a, 34-35
6th Sunday of Easter	Jn 14:15-21	Jn 15:9-17	Jn 14:23-29
Ascension of Our Lord	Mt 28:16-20	Mk 16:15-20	Lk 24:46-53
7th Sunday of Easter	Jn 17:1-11a	Jn 17:11b-19	Jn 17:20-26
Pentecost Vigil	Jn 7:37-39	Jn 7:37-39	Jn 7:37-39
Pentecost Day	Jn 20:19-23	Jn 20:19-23	Jn 20:19-23
Trinity Sunday	Jn 3:16-18	Mt 28:16-20	Jn 16:12-15
Corpus Christi	Jn 6:51-58	Mk 14:12-16, 22-26	Lk 9:11b-17
Sacred Heart of Jesus	Mt 11:25-30	Jn 19:31-37	Lk 15:3-7
1st Sunday in Ordinary Time	Mt 3:13-17	Mk 1:6b-11	Lk 3:15-16, 21-22

2nd Sunday	Jn 1:29-34	Jn 1:35-42	Jn 2:1-12
3rd Sunday	Mt 4:12-23	Mk 1:14-20	Lk 1:1-4; 4:14-21
4th Sunday	Mt 5:1-12a	Mk 1:21-28	Lk 4:21-30
5th Sunday	Mt 5:13-16	Mk 1:29-39	Lk 5:1-11
6th Sunday	Mt 5:17-37	Mk 1:40-45	Lk 6:17, 20-26
7th Sunday	Mt 5:38-48	Mk 2:1-12	Lk 6:27-38
8th Sunday	Mt 6:24-34	Mk 2:18-22	Lk 6:39-45
9th Sunday	Mt 7:21-27	Mk 2:23---3:6	Lk 7:1-10
10th Sunday	Mt 9:9-13	Mk 3:20-35	Lk 7:11-17
11th Sunday	Mt 9:36–10:8	Mk 4:26–34	Lk 7:36–8:3
12th Sunday	Mt 10:26-33	Mk 4:35-41	Lk 9:18-24
13th Sunday	Mt 10:37-42	Mk 5:21-43	Lk 9:51-62
14th Sunday	Mt 11:25-30	Mk 6:1-6	Lk 10:1-12, 17–20
15th Sunday	Mt 13:1-23	Mk 6:7-13	Lk 10:25-37
16th Sunday	Mt 13:24-43	Mk 6:30-34	Lk 10:38-42
17th Sunday	Mt 13:44-52	Jn 6:1-15	Lk 11:1-13
18th Sunday	Mt 14:13-21	Jn 6:24-35	Lk 12:13-31
19th Sunday	Mt 14:22-33	Jn 6:41-45	Lk 12:32-48
20th Sunday	Mt 15:21-28	Jn 6:51-58	Lk 12:49-53
21st Sunday	Mt 16:13-20	Jn 6:60-69	Lk 13:22-30
22nd Sunday	Mt 16:21-27	Mk 7: 1-8, 14-15, 21-23	Lk 14:1, 7-14
23rd Sunday	Mt 18:15-20	Mk 7:31-37	Lk 14:25-33
24th Sunday	Mt 18:21-35	Mk 8:27-35	Lk 15:1-32
25th Sunday	Mt 20:1-16a	Mk 9:30-37	Lk 16:1-13
26th Sunday	Mt 21:28-32	Mk 9:38-43, 45, 47-48	Lk 16:19-31
27th Sunday	Mt 21:33-43	Mk 10:2-16	Lk 17:5-10
28th Sunday	Mt 22:1-14	Mk 10:17-30	Lk 17:11-19
29th Sunday	Mt 22:15-21	Mk 10:35-43	Lk 18:1-8
30th Sunday	Mt 22:34-40	Mk 10:46-53	Lk 18:9-14
31st Sunday	Mt 23:1-12	Mk 12:28b-34	Lk 19:1-10

32nd Sunday	Mt 25:1-13	Mk 12:38-44	Lk 20:27-38
33rd Sunday	Mt 25:14-30	Mk 13:24-32	Lk 21:5-19
Christ the King	Mt 25:31-46	Jn 18:33b-37	Lk 23:35-43

Sunday and Feast Day Gospel Reading Cycle
Universal Lectionary

(Used by the Episcopal, Lutheran, Presbyterian, United Church of Christ and Methodist Churches)

Sunday or Holy Day	1st Year or Year A	2nd Year or Year B	3rd Year or Year C
1st Sunday of Advent	Mt 24:37-44	Mk 13:(24-32) 33-37	Lk 21:25-31
2nd Sunday of Advent	Mt 3:1-12	Mk 1:1-8	Lk 3:1-6
3rd Sunday of Advent	Mt 11:2-11	Jn 1:6-8, 19-28 or Jn 3:23-30	Lk 3:7-18
4th Sunday of Advent	Mt 1:18-25	Lk 1:26-38	Lk 1:35-49 (50-56)
Christmas Day I	Lk 2:1-14 (15-20)	Lk 2:1-14 (15-20)	Lk 2:1-14 (15-20)
Christmas Day II	Lk 2:(1-14) (15-20)	Lk 2:(1-14) (15-20)	Lk 2:(1-14) (15-20)
Christmas Day III	Jn 1:1-14	Jn 1:1-14	Jn 1:1-14
First Sunday After Christmas	Jn 1:1-18	Jn 1:1-18	Jn 1:1-18
January 1, (Holy Name)	Lk 2:15-21	Lk 2:15-21	Lk 2:15-21
2nd Sunday After Christmas	Mt 2:13-15, 19-23 or Lk 2:41-52 or Mt 2:1-12	Mt 2:13-15, 19-23 or Lk 2:41-52 or Mt 2:1-12	Mt 2:13-15, 19-23 or Lk 2:41-52 or Mt 2:1-12
Epiphany	Mt 2:1-12	Mt 2:1-12	Mt 2:1-12
1st Sunday After Epiphany	Mt 3:13-17	Mk 1:7-11	Lk 3:15-16, 21-22
2nd Sunday After Epiphany	Jn 1:29-41	Jn 1:43-51	Jn 2:1-11

3rd Sunday After Epiphany	Mt 4:12-23	Mk 1:14-20	Lk 4:14-21
4th Sunday After Epiphany	Mt 5:1-12	Mk 1:21-28	Lk 4:21-32
5th Sunday After Epiphany	Mt 5:13-20	Mk 1:29-39	Lk 5:1-11
6th Sunday After Epiphany	Mt 5:21-24, 27-30, 33-37	Mk 1:40-45	Lk 6:17-26
7th Sunday After Epiphany	Mt 5:38-48	Mk 2:1-12	Lk 6:27-38
8th Sunday After Epiphany	Mt 6:24-34	Mk 2:18-22	Lk 6:39-49
Last Sunday After Epiphany	Mt 17:1-9	Mk 9:2-9	Lk 9:28-36
Ash Wednesday	Mt 6:1-6, 16-21	Mt 6:1-6, 16-21	Mt 6:1-6, 16-21
1st Sunday of Lent	Mt 4:1-11	Mk 1:9-13	Lk 4:1-13
2nd Sunday of Lent	Jn 3:1-17	Mk 8:31-38	Lk 13:(22-30) 31-35
3rd Sunday of Lent	Jn 4:5-26 (27-38) 39-42	Jn 2:13-22	Lk 13:1-9
4th Sunday of Lent	Jn 9:1-13 (14-27) 28-38	Jn 6:4-15	Lk 15:11-32
5th Sunday of Lent	Jn 11:(1-17) 18-44	Jn 12:20-33	Lk 20:9-19
Palm Sunday	Mt (26:36-75) 27:1-54(55-66)	Mk (14:32-72) 15:1-39(40-47)	Lk (22:39-71) 23:1-49(50-56)
Maundy Thursday	Jn 13:1-15 or Lk:22 14-30	Jn 13:1-15 or Lk 22:14-30	Jn 13:1-15 or Lk 22:14-30
Good Friday	Jn (18:1-40) 19:1-37	Jn (18:1-40) 19:1-37	Jn (18:1-40) 19:1-37
Holy Saturday	Mt 27:57-66 or Jn 19:38-42	Mt 27:57-66 or Jn 19:38-42	Mt 27:57-66 or Jn 19:38-42

Easter Day-Early Service	Mt 28:1-10	Mt 28:1-10	Mt 28:1-10
Easter Day- Principal Service	Jn 20:1-10 (11-18) or Mt 28:1-10	Mk 16:1-8	Lk 24:1-10
Easter Day- Evening Service	Lk 24:13-35	Lk 24:13-35	Lk 24:13-35
2nd Sunday of Easter	Jn 20:19-31	Jn 20:19-31	Jn 20:19-31
3rd Sunday of Easter	Lk 24:13-35	Lk 24:36b-48	Jn 21:1-14
4th Sunday of Easter	Jn 10:1-10	Jn 10:11-16	Jn 10:22-30
5th Sunday of Easter	Jn 14:1-14	Jn 14:15-21	Jn 13:31-35
6th Sunday of Easter	Jn 15:1-8	Jn 15:9-17	Jn 14:23-29
Ascension Day	Lk 24:49-53 or Mk 16:9-15, 19-20	Lk 24:49-53 or Mk 16:9-15, 19-20	Lk 24:49-53 or Mk 16:9-15, 19-20
7th Sunday of Easter	Jn 17:1-11	Jn 17:11b-19	Jn 17:11b-19
Pentecost Vigil	Jn 7:37-39a	Jn 7:37-39a	Jn 7:37-39a
Pentecost Day	Jn 20:19-23 or Jn:14:8-17	Jn 20:19-23 or Jn 14:8-17	Jn 20:19-23 or Jn 14:8-17
Trinity Sunday	Mt 28:16-20	Jn 3:1-16	Jn 16:(5-11) 12-15
Proper 1	Mt 5:21-24, 27-30, 33-37	Mk 1:40-45	Lk 6:17-26
Proper 2	Mt 5:38-48	Mk 2:1-12	Lk 6:27-38
Proper 3	Mt 6:24-34	Mk 2:18-22	Lk 6:39-49
Proper 4	Mt 7:21-27	Mk 2:23-28	Lk 7:1-10
Proper 5	Mt 9:9-13	Mk 3:20-35	Lk 7:11-17
Proper 6	Mt 9:35–10:8 (9-15)	Mk 4:26-34	Lk 7:36-50
Proper 7	Mt 10:(16-23) 24-33	Mk 4:35-41; (5:1-20)	Lk 9:18-24
Proper 8	Mt 10:34-42	Mk 5:22-24, 35b-43	Lk 9:51-62

Proper 9	Mt 11:25-30	Mk 6:1-6	Lk 10:1-12, 16-20
Proper 10	Mt 13:1-9, 18-23	Mk 6:7-13	Lk 10:25-37
Proper 11	Mt 13:24-30, 36-43	Mk 6:30-44	Lk 10:38-42
Proper 12	Mt 13:31-33, 44-49a	Mk 6:45-52	Lk 11:1-13
Proper 13	Mt 14:13-21	Jn 6:24-35	Lk 12:13-21
Proper 14	Mt 14:22-33	Jn 6:37-51	Lk 12:32-40
Proper 15	Mt 15:21-28	Jn 6:53-59	Lk 12:49-56
Proper 16	Mt 16:13-20	Jn 6:60-69	Lk 13:22-30
Proper 17	Mt 16:21-27	Mk 7: 1-8, 14-15, 21-23	Lk 14:1,7-14
Proper 18	Mt 18:15-20	Mk 7:31-37	Lk 14:25-33
Proper 19	Mt 18:21-35	Mk 8:27-38 or Mk 9:14-29	Lk 15:1-10
Proper 20	Mt 20:1-16	Mk 9:30-37	Lk 16:1-13
Proper 21	Mt 21:28-32	Mk 9:38-43, 45, 47-48	Lk 16:19-31
Proper 22	Mt 21:33-43	Mk 10:2-9	Lk 17:5-10
Proper 23	Mt 22:1-14	Mk 10:17-27 (28-31)	Lk 17:11-19
Proper 24	Mt 22:15-21	Mk 10:35-45	Lk 18:1-8a
Proper 25	Mt 22:34-46	Mk 10:46-52	Lk 18:9-14
Proper 26	Mt 23:1-12	Mk 12:28-34	Lk 19:1-10
Proper 27	Mt 25:1-13	Mk 12:38-44	Lk 20:27 (28-33) 34-38
Proper 28	Mt 25:14-15, 19-29	Mk 13:14-23	Lk 21:5-19
Proper 29	Mt 25:31-46	Jn 18:33-37 or Mk 11:1-11	Lk 19:29-38

APPENDIX B

Variations in the Opening Line of Psalm 22

Three major variations exist with the opening line of Psalm 22.

The Gospel of Matthew: 27:46 quotes the line in Hebrew as, "Eli, Eli, lema sabachthani?" Matthew wanted to make the connection between the name Eli, a name for God, and the prophet Elijah.

The Gospel of Mark 15:34 quotes the line in Aramaic as, "Eloi, Eloi, lema sabachthani?"

Current Hebrew texts translate the line: "Eliy, Eliy, lema azabetani."

ACKNOWLEDGEMENTS

Book One and Book Two are the culmination of my faith and prayer and life to this point. Every person whose path I've crossed, and who has crossed mine, has shaped this work and me. Family, friend and opponent—your contribution is here. I bow with gratitude.

An Arabic proverb says, "Seek not to know what the ancients knew, seek to know their source." To my greatest teachers—Morton Kelsey, John Sanford, Henri Nouwen, John Dunne, Raymond Brown, James Dunning, Christianne Brusselsman, Joseph Campbell, Dora Kalff, Claudio Rise, Kay Bradway, Nessie Bayley, Eva Maria Sanchez, my sitto and jiddo, parents, aunts and uncles, brothers and nephews, great-niece and cousins—your hearts touched mine. You taught me to listen beyond words, and to go beyond your words.

I am grateful to many authors and scholars beginning with the writings of C.G. Jung and ending with that of Robin Griffith-Jones. Their work provided the intellectual constructs to the re-discovery of the four gospels as quadratos. As their thinking served mine, I hope that these books may enable you to go beyond my thoughts.

St. Exupéry said, "What is most essential in life is friendship." No one has been a better friend to this work than Michelle Gaugy. She has been wise counselor and exquisite editor. Many times she knew the gospels better than I. Her home served as the birthplace of the name *quadratos*. And to everything she added beauty.

Alongside Michelle's efforts have been the critical thinking, eagle-eyes and gracious hands of Connie Cox, Andrea Horner, Sheri Swanson and Josie Abbenante. They kept me on the path from earliest days to final hour. Thanks to Peter Honsberger, CEO of Cold Tree Press, whose good humor, "can do" attitude and evident skill made the difference. To this incredible circle—your faith humbles my heart, and challenges me to live quadratos with each breath.

At critical junctures, angels—many angels—pointed the way:

Bob and Linda Shumate, Larry Greenberg and Carol Kindschi, Sylvia Boorstein, Maggie and John Monroe-Cassel, Michael and Geraldine Gospe, Betsy Caprio and Thomas Hedberg, J.L. and Sharon Shaia, Tessamarie and David Capitolo, Betty and Emma Jackson, Caroline Isaacs and Randy Mayers, Christy Sweeny, Marilyn Penny, Padma Catell, Thomas Grady, Bob and Charleen Roccucci, Maura Power, Mirabai Starr, Nahum Ward-Lev, Glenda Elliott, Paula Pointer, Joseph Mitchell, Cynthia Gray, Joe Cieszinkski, Richard Murphy, Peggy Garrett, William and Mary Faye Shaia, Julie Davis, Cil Braun, Bunnie Graham, Trudy and Larry Rankin, Andy and Lilla Weinberger, Pamela Burnham, Peter Abbott, Steve and Karen Liechti, Jack Kornfield, John Livingston, Jim Adelmann, Gita Morena, John Shaia, Sandra Lommasson, Jean Holsten, David Elliott, Jennifer and Andrew Greenberg, Anne Ritchings and Kay Hankinson, Nancy and Robert Ullrey, Anne Noss, Marianne Lewis, Cherie Porter, Jan Richardson, Lee Ben-Yehuda, Jean Richardson, Brendalyn Batchelor, Robert Lentz, Melody Bolen, Jananne Lovett-Keen, Karl Tinsley, Vera and Bill Roughton, Maria Padilla, Patricia Stanley, Gail Helgeson, Marjorie Hoyer-Smith, Kathy Anuzczyk, Kathy Carey, Susan Rush, Darcy and Robert Wharton, JeanAnne and Jim Swope, Sanae Nakamura, Lydia Lennihan and Steve Wong, Edie Green, Krisanne Bender, JR Lancaster, Francis Wade, Michiel Crawford, Oleta Saunders, Thomas Williams, Woody

Wiggins, Virginia Hall, Barbara Beasley-Murphy, Anita Ahuja, Joan and Bill Hanrahan, Jan Patterson, Paul Mark Schwan, Joyce Hansen, Michelle and Greg Pfister, Suzanne Toolan, David Mullen, George Wenzinger and Colleen Gregg.

To this great and diverse chorus, I shout, "Jeru-Shalom." Sing on!

The four gospels were born in community prayer. So too this work. The weekly lectio meditation communities at Christ the King Retreat Center in Citrus Heights, CA and the Blue Door Retreat in Santa Fe, NM have been mid-wife and Spirit-vessel of these books. Through the easy and difficult years, they have held me in prayer. To you, who have faithfully gathered to pray the Gospels in the ancient sequence, may your hearts be edified by this work—it is truly the gift that has come from your lives, wisdom and grace.

And to the many individuals who answered the call to support this work and to be part of the Beloved Community—your names are inscribed at the Blue Door Retreat and on my heart. May your every step be filled with the *shalom* of quadratos well journeyed.

RESOURCES

www.quadratos.com

For information on Quadratos, including ordering books, books on CD, audiotapes and supplemental materials, as well as details on Dr. Shaia's upcoming book signings, speaking engagements, workshops and retreats.

---

www.bluedoorretreat.com

Plan a retreat or a contemplative vacation at the Blue Door Retreat (featured on the PBS series, *Boomers*) in Santa Fe, New Mexico. You may also arrange for an individual or group retreat/seminar with Dr. Shaia.

Contact Dr. Shaia

Please email: *drshaia@quadratos.com*

All comments—including heyokas and suggestions—are welcome.
Thank You.

Printed in the United States
102161LV00007B/154-756/A

9 781583 850435